Stories OF GRACE

VOLUME 2: NEW TESTAMENT BIBLE CHARACTERS

Children's **MINISTRY** Curriculum

First published in 2015 by Striving Together Publications, a ministry of Lancaster Baptist Church, Lancaster, CA 93535. Striving Together Publications is committed to providing tried, trusted, and proven books that will further equip local churches to carry out the Great Commission. Your comments and suggestions are valued.

Striving Together Publications
4020 E. Lancaster Blvd.
Lancaster, CA 93535
800.201.7748

Written by Joanne Bass
Cover design by Andrew Jones
Layout by Amy Daufen
Layout design by Craig Parker
Contributors:

Terrie Chappell   Alyssa Lofgren
Danielle Mordh   Tracy Dizon

ISBN 978-1-59894-296-5
Printed in the United States of America

Contents

How to Use This Curriculum

Stories of Grace

This manual is Volume 2 of a larger series, *Stories of Grace*. The complete series provides a four-quarter, fifty-two lesson resource. Together, all four volumes in this set are as follows:

- Volume 1: Old Testament Bible Characters
- Volume 2: New Testament Bible Characters
- Volume 3: Animals and Objects Used by God
- Volume 4: Behind the Scenes Bible Helpers

For a complete scope and sequence chart, listing the Bible stories and lessons presented in each volume, visit strivingtogether.com/storiesofgrace.

A Series of Thirteen Lessons

This teacher manual contains thirteen lessons, each focusing on the life of one of thirteen prominent characters in the New Testament. Each lesson contains a riveting story and emphasizes an applicable truth for children. Lessons are thoroughly supplemented with biblical references, teaching resources, and creative ideas.

Class Time

Each lesson contains sufficient resources to fill a ninety-minute class period. For those attempting to use the curriculum for a sixty-minute class period, we suggest the teacher choose which resources would be most effective and use them accordingly.

Age Appropriateness

This curriculum and its accompanying resources have been written for use with elementary-age children. Those who teach preschool-age children will also find it compatible for use with ages four and under.

Ideas & Resources Included

Experts suggest that we can estimate the average child's attention span as one minute per year of life. So for example, those teaching eight-year-olds should expect to change activities in the classroom every eight minutes or so to keep the students' attention. The one exception to this rule would be the main Bible lesson itself. During the Bible lesson, attention can be kept through the combined use of visual aids such as flash cards, objects, role-play, digital projection, and a chalk/dry-erase board.

Included in Every Lesson:

One-Page Lesson Snapshot

At the beginning of each lesson is a summary page, intended to be photocopied by the teacher and tucked into his or her Bible for ready reference. This page may also be distributed to the assistant teachers in advance, so they may prepare for their classroom responsibilities. This page includes each week's lesson title, Scripture references, memory verse, lesson outline, and a suggested class schedule.

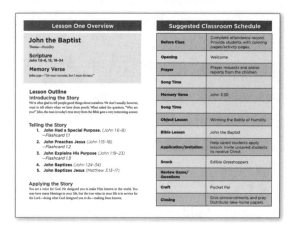

Teacher's Checklist

Use the weekly checklist to gather the appropriate materials in preparation for Sunday. Instructions may be given to an assistant teacher to pick up the needed items for the suggested craft, snack, game, or object lesson. The checklist identifies additional items found on the Ministry Resource download (sold separately).

Snack Suggestion

Children will enjoy a different snack each week, which will not only be a treat but also a reminder of the truth learned. This is a fun and tasty way to give children a break during their time in the classroom.

Scripture Passage

Great teaching begins with God's Word! Teachers should study the included Scripture passage numerous times throughout the week, make notes, and become familiar with the passage.

Lesson Introduction

In many lessons, thought-provoking questions are asked at the beginning so students may consider their own real-life circumstances, similar to those they will encounter in the Scripture. As you begin these lessons, allow for a brief period of answers and open discussion.

Bible Lesson

Each lesson surveys a select portion of Scripture, taking a walk of discovery through the biblical record. Lessons are divided into easy-to-identify points with helpful cross-references included. As each story develops, we offer possibilities of daily routines and feelings for each character based on the context of Scripture. These contextual illustrations are used to support the theme of the lesson and are not taken directly from Scripture.

Lesson Application

At the conclusion of each lesson, the teacher should seek to remind students of one or two primary truths to take away from the story. Then ask, in practical terms, how children might apply those truths during the week. At this time in the lesson, students who would like to receive Christ as Saviour should be encouraged to speak to a trained counselor.

Review Game with Questions

A unique, theme-oriented game is included in each lesson for the purpose of review. While other questions may be added by the teacher, a list of initial review questions designed to reinforce the lesson are provided for use during the game.

Teaching the Memory Verse

A creative way of teaching the week's memory verse is included in each lesson. The Visual Resource Packet (sold separately) includes visuals for use with each memory verse. These visuals are also available on the Ministry Resource download (sold separately).

Object Lesson

Children will remember the five-minute object lessons designed to support the Bible lesson. Each object lesson is easy to teach and simple to prepare using objects most of us have at home or that are available at a retail store.

Craft

Each lesson includes a craft that students and parents will enjoy putting on display! The craft section includes a supply list, easy-to-follow directions, and simple thoughts on how it relates to the Bible lesson.

Teaching Tips

Creative ideas and suggestions are provided for the purpose of effectively delivering the truths contained in each week's lesson.

Teacher's Note

Historical notes, practical instructions, and biblical definitions are provided to assist the teacher in study and preparation.

Suggested Visual Aids:

The "mixing up" of the weekly visuals will keep students engaged and will prevent predictability.

Flash Cards

In the thirteen lessons, flash cards are used to illustrate the Bible story (three cards for each story). Find the arrow in the lesson margin to show the flash card to the students at the appropriate time. These thirty-nine flash cards are included in the Visual Resource Packet (sold separately).

Act It Out

In certain lessons, we suggest selecting students to help "act out" the Bible story. Vary your choices to give all students wishing to be involved the opportunity to do so throughout the course of the series. The students more eager to participate in this role play are likely those who will benefit most from the exercise.

Use an Object

Some weeks, teachers may utilize a physical object to keep students' attention. Suggested props of this nature are found at strategic points in the margin of the Bible lesson.

Draw It!

Many classrooms are equipped with a chalk or dry-erase board. Included in the margin of select lessons are simple sketches that even the most artistically-challenged teacher can draw. We suggest that you have the students draw along with you to reinforce the events taking place in the story.

The Ministry Resource Download:

We recommend that each church or class purchase the Ministry Resource download and make the files available to as many teachers as desired. This enables the investment in the download to be spread over an unlimited volume and time.

Coloring Pages

Younger children (roughly three-year-olds through third grade) will enjoy coloring a scene from each week's Bible lesson. Share an original copy with each teacher and provide as many photocopies as needed for all classes, one per student.

Activity Pages

Older children (roughly 3rd through 6th grades) will enjoy creative activities related to each week's Bible lesson. Activities include word searches, crossword puzzles, mazes, and brainteasers. Share an original copy with each teacher and provide as many photocopies as needed for all classes, one per student.

Student Take-Home Paper

The take-home paper is designed to help students take the Bible truth into the week ahead as they leave the classroom. Take-home papers will remind students of the weekly memory verse, include additional review questions, and suggest practical ways for applying the lesson in everyday experiences. Share an original copy with each teacher and provide as many photocopies as needed for all classes, one per student.

PowerPoint Presentation

A Microsoft PowerPoint presentation is available for each of the thirteen lessons. If you have a television, computer monitor, or projector available, children will enjoy being able to follow the main points of the lesson on the screen. Each week's memory verse is also included in the presentation. These presentations are fully editable, and may be shared with as many teachers as desired. Feel free to add or edit slides as you wish.

Memory Verse Visuals

The same visuals included in the Visual Resource Packet are included in PDF form on the Ministry Resource download. These are provided so that teachers may use the images in projection or another form, including providing copies to students.

Craft and Game Templates

Throughout the series, templates are utilized with select crafts and games. These templates are found on the Ministry Resource download in PDF form.

Suggested Classroom Schedule

Before Class		Complete attendance record. Provide students with coloring pages/activity pages.
Opening		Welcome
Prayer		Prayer requests and praise reports from the children
Song Time		
Memory Verse		John 3:30
Song Time		
Object Lesson		Winning the Battle of Humility
Bible Lesson		John the Baptist
Application/Invitation		Help saved students apply lesson. Invite unsaved students to receive Christ.
Snack		Edible Grasshoppers
Review Game/ Questions		
Craft		Pocket Pal
Closing		Give announcements and pray. Distribute take-home papers.

Lesson One Overview

John the Baptist
Theme—Humility

Scripture
John 1:6-8, 15, 19-34

Memory Verse
John 3:30—*"He must increase, but I must decrease."*

Lesson Outline
Introducing the Story
We're often glad to tell people good things about ourselves. We don't usually, however, want to tell others when we have done poorly. When asked the question, "Who are you?" John, the man in today's true story from the Bible gave a very interesting answer.

Telling the Story
1. **John Had a Special Purpose.** *(John 1:6-8)*
   —*Flashcard 1.1*

2. **John Preaches Jesus** *(John 1:15-18)*
   —*Flashcard 1.2*

3. **John Explains His Purpose** *(John 1:19-23)*
   —*Flashcard 1.3*

4. **John Baptizes** *(John 1:24-34)*

5. **John Baptizes Jesus** *(Matthew 3:13-17)*

Applying the Story
You are a voice for God. He designed you to make Him known to the world. You may have many blessings in your life, but the true value in your life is in service for the Lord—doing what God designed you to do—making Jesus known.

LESSON ONE
John the Baptist

1

Theme: Humility

TEACHER'S CHECKLIST

- ❑ Read John 1:6–8, 15, 19–34.
- ❑ Study Lesson One.
- ❑ Flash cards 1.1–1.3.
- ❑ Prepare snack—Edible Grasshoppers.
- ❑ Gather for object lesson—**boxing gloves.**
- ❑ Gather for review game—several balloons, push pins divided into three labeled containers, a bag for the push pin containers.
- ❑ **Gather for craft—printables from Ministry Resource download, double sided tape, magnet stickers.**
- ❑ Print Memory Verse Flashcards from the Ministry Resource download.
- ❑ **Print and duplicate Coloring Pages or Activity Pages on the Ministry Resource download (one per student).**
- ❑ **Print and duplicate the Take-Home Paper on the Ministry Resource download (one per student).**

SCRIPTURES

John 1:6–8, 15, 19–34

6   There was a man sent from God, whose name was John.

7   The same came for a witness, to bear witness of the Light, that all men through him might believe.

8   He was not that Light, but was sent to bear witness of that Light.

15 John bare witness of him, and cried, saying, This was he of whom I spake, He that cometh after me is preferred before me: for he was before me.

19 And this is the record of John, when the Jews sent priests and Levites from Jerusalem to ask him, Who art thou?

20 And he confessed, and denied not; but confessed, I am not the Christ.

21 And they asked him, What then? Art thou Elias? And he saith, I am not. Art thou that prophet? And he answered, No.

22 Then said they unto him, Who art thou? that we may give an answer to them that sent us. What sayest thou of thyself?

23 He said, I am the voice of one crying in the wilderness, Make straight the way of the Lord, as said the prophet Esaias.

24 And they which were sent were of the Pharisees.

25 And they asked him, and said unto him, Why baptizest thou then, if thou be not that Christ, nor Elias, neither that prophet?

26 John answered them, saying, I baptize with water: but there standeth one among you, whom ye know not;

27 He it is, who coming after me is preferred before me, whose shoe's latchet I am not worthy to unloose.

28 These things were done in Bethabara beyond Jordan, where John was baptizing.

29 The next day John seeth Jesus coming unto him, and saith, Behold the Lamb of God, which taketh away the sin of the world.

30 This is he of whom I said, After me cometh a man which is preferred before me: for he was before me.

31 And I knew him not: but that he should be made manifest to Israel, therefore am I come baptizing with water.

32 And John bare record, saying, I saw the Spirit descending from heaven like a dove, and it abode upon him.

33 And I knew him not: but he that sent me to baptize with water, the same said unto me, Upon whom thou shalt see the Spirit descending, and remaining on him, the same is he which baptizeth with the Holy Ghost.

34 And I saw, and bare record that this is the Son of God.

Introducing the Story

If someone were to ask you, "Who are you?" how would you answer them? (Allow students to answer.) You would likely tell them your name—"I am Mrs./Mr. _____. Or, I am Samantha Jones. Or, I am Tyler Smith.

Maybe you would tell them something about yourself. "I am Drew Anderson, and I am on the soccer team." Or, "I am Ashley Williams, and I love to shop." Or, "I am Kaylee Evans, and I am in honors classes at school."

We could say many things about ourselves, because we all have many activities in our lives—activities at home, at church, at school, and other places. We all have parts of our lives about which we are happy to share details, and parts of our lives we would rather not talk about.

We're often glad to tell about a good report card, coming in first in a race, or being chosen for some honor.

We don't usually, however, want to tell others that we did poorly on a test, came in last in a competition, or that we were caught in a lie.

Whether we feel like we have been successful, or whether we feel we have failed, those of us who are Christians always have something we can be glad to share about ourselves—I am _____, and I am a Christian!

When asked the question, "Who are you?" John, the man in today's true story from the Bible, gave a very interesting answer.

The Story

1. John Had a Special Purpose (John 1:6–8)

John was a man with a very special purpose. The Old Testament prophets, Isaiah and Malachi, had written about John hundreds of years earlier. Before John was even born, an angel told his father about the special purpose for his life—to tell people to be ready for the Saviour who was coming. The angel said that many people will turn to the Saviour because of his son's message.

Luke 1:16

16   And many of the children of Israel shall he turn to the Lord their God.

Because John's purpose was so special, the angel told Zacharias that he was to make sure his child lived a life totally dedicated to God. The angel gave Zacharias and Elisabeth instructions to follow.

Zacharias and Elisabeth did what the angel said. As they raised John in their home, they were careful to teach him God's ways. They loved God, and they wanted others to see how good and how holy God is when they saw their son John.

As John grew older, he chose God's ways for himself. John loved God, and he wanted others to see how good and how holy God is when they looked at John.

John spent much time in the wilderness, where he could be alone with God and hear God's voice in his heart.

Luke 1:80

80   And the child grew, and waxed strong in spirit, and was in the deserts till the day of his shewing unto Israel.

> **TEACHER'S NOTE**
>
> John and his message were a fulfillment of the prophecy, "The voice of him that crieth in the wilderness, Prepare ye the way of the Lord, make straight in the desert a highway for our God" (Isaiah 40:3).
>
> "As it is written in the prophets, Behold, I send my messenger before thy face, which shall prepare thy way before thee. The voice of one crying in the wilderness, Prepare ye the way of the Lord, make his paths straight." (Mark 1:2–3)

Flash Card 1.1

In the wilderness, John learned to survive with what was available. He wore a simple, rough robe made from camel's hair, tied together with a leather belt around his waist. His food was simple too—wild honey and locusts.

Mark 1:6

6   And John was clothed with camel's hair, and with a girdle of a skin about his loins; and he did eat locusts and wild honey;

There was something else special about John—he was the second cousin of Jesus, and he was only six months older than Jesus. His mother and Jesus' mother were cousins.

If someone were to ask John the question, "Who are you?" he certainly would have a lot to brag about—he was Jesus' second cousin, his life had been prophesied hundreds of years before he was born, and an angel prepared his father to raise him according to God's instructions!

2. John Preaches Jesus (John 1:15–18)

One day, when he was about thirty years old, John heard God telling him it was time to go share the good news that Jesus had come to be the Saviour from sin.

Luke 3:2b–3

2   …the word of God came unto John the son of Zacharias in the wilderness.

3   And he came into all the country about Jordan, preaching the baptism of repentance for the remission of sins;

Flash Card 1.2

And so he went. He went through the whole countryside preaching and teaching about Jesus. Many people went into the wilderness to hear John preach.

"I have come to tell you that the Messiah—the Saviour who God promised would come to save us from our sins—has come. He is the true Light of the world.

"He is coming after me, but He is greater than me. Even though He comes after me, He was before me. He always was, because He is God the Son. Believe on the Saviour."

3. John Explains His Purpose (John 1:19–23)

The Jewish religious leaders were jealous of the Messiah who was coming. They were afraid that people would follow Him, instead of following them. They sent messengers to John. "And just who are you?" they asked.

John loved Jesus so much, and he was so in tune to his purpose of making Christ known, that he didn't say one word about himself. He didn't say, "I'm the second cousin of the Saviour. My purpose was prophesied in the Old Testament—I'm sure you've read about me. An angel told my father about my purpose before I was even born." Instead, he told them that he was preparing the way for the Messiah.

"Then who are you?" the Jews asked. "What do you have to say for yourself?" In fact, John seemed to know God the Father so well, that the Jews wondered if John was the Messiah.

"Are you the Christ?" they asked him.

Luke 3:15

15   And as the people were in expectation, and all men mused in their hearts of John, whether he were the Christ, or not;

"No," John answered. "I'm just a voice. I'm simply here to tell you to get ready for the Messiah—the One who has come to save us from our sins. The prophet Malachi told us someone would come to prepare us for the Saviour, and I am the one he was talking about. I'm nobody special, but you should listen to me, because I am God's messenger to tell you, 'Get ready for the Saviour!'"

4. John Baptizes (John 1:24–34)

"If you are not the Christ, why do you baptize people?" the Pharisees wanted to know. (After all, John baptized so many people that he was known as John the Baptist.)

"I baptize with water. When someone is baptized by me, they are showing on the outside that they have changed on the inside. That's all I do.

"But the Messiah is coming after me. He is so much greater than I am. I am not worthy to even perform the duty of a servant for Him—I'm not worthy to stoop down and loose the strap of his sandal.

"When He comes, He will baptize you on the inside—He will send the Holy Spirit to live in the hearts of those who trust Him as their Saviour."

> ◀ **Flash Card 1.3**
>
> **TEACHER'S NOTE**
>
> The Bible teaches that baptism is a symbol of what has happened on the inside of a person. God wants every Christian to be baptized to show others that he/she has trusted Jesus.
>
> Some people teach that baptism washes away sins, but the Bible teaches that the only way for sins to be forgiven, or washed away, is by trusting in the blood Jesus shed when He died on the cross. Baptism, or anything other than Jesus' blood, cannot wash away our sins. It is only through trusting in Jesus as Saviour that we are saved from our sins.
>
> Hebrews 9:22b "without shedding of blood is no remission."
>
> You may wish to use the illustration of two people getting married. The wedding rings they exchange don't make them married—they simply show others that they are married. Likewise, baptism shows others that we have trusted Jesus.
>
> If baptism's purpose were to wash away sins, the Father would not have wanted Jesus to be baptized, because Jesus never sinned.

5. John Baptizes Jesus (Matthew 3:13–17)

One day Jesus came to the Jordan River, where John was baptizing. After John had baptized the last person there, Jesus stepped to the edge of the river and asked John to baptize Him.

> **Luke 3:21**
>
> 21   Now when all the people were baptized, it came to pass, that Jesus also being baptized, and praying, the heaven was opened,

"Oh, no, Jesus!" John said. "I'm not worthy to baptize you. I should be baptized by you—why are you coming to me?!"

"The right thing for me to do is to do everything God the Father has planned for those who follow Him to do," Jesus answered.

John did what Jesus asked—he baptized Jesus, the Saviour of the world. And, when Jesus came up out of the water, a glorious voice from Heaven spoke, "This is my beloved Son, in whom I am well pleased." God the Father was pleased with His Son.

"This man—Jesus—truly is the Son of God," John exclaimed.

> **John 1:34**
>
> 34   And I saw, and bare record that this is the Son of God.

Applying The Story

John had many things he could have been proud of. He could have been proud that his life had been written about in the Bible hundreds of years before he was born. He could have been proud that he was the cousin of Jesus Christ. He could have been proud that he lived a life totally dedicated to God—that he didn't do many things others did. He could have been proud that an angel had told his father how to raise him. He could have been proud that Jesus wanted him to baptize Him.

But, when the Pharisees asked John who he was, what did he tell them? (Allow students to answer.) He said, "I am not that Christ." He didn't want people to think of him at all—he only wanted to point people to Jesus.

The amazing thing is that God said, "Of every single person that had ever been born, no one was greater than John the Baptist."

Matthew 11:11

11 Verily I say unto you, Among them that are born of women there hath not risen a greater than John the Baptist: notwithstanding he that is least in the kingdom of heaven is greater than he.

Think about some of the people who had already been born when Jesus made that statement:

- Abraham was the first Hebrew (Israelite)—he is called the father of the Jewish nation. God spoke to Abraham. Abraham had great faith in God, and he walked with God. Abraham let God be in control of everything he had. The Bible even calls Abraham the "friend of God." But God said that Abraham was not greater than John the Baptist.

James 2:23

23 And the scripture was fulfilled which saith, Abraham believed God, and it was imputed unto him for righteousness: and he was called the Friend of God.

- Moses was the man God chose to rescue the children of Israel from being slaves in Egypt and lead them (and there were millions of them!) to the land God had promised to them. Moses was selected by God to teach and train the children of Israel God's laws. Moses was one of the greatest men who ever lived. But God said that Moses was not greater than John the Baptist.

- David was amazingly brave and courageous. As a teenager he killed a lion and a bear with his own hands to protect his sheep. Later he killed the giant Goliath to protect the Israelites and to protect God's name. David fought many battles and loved God with all his heart. In fact, the Bible calls David "a man after [God's] own heart." But God said that David was not greater than John the Baptist.

Acts 13:22

22 And when he had removed him, he raised up unto them David to be their king; to whom also he gave testimony, and said, I have found David the son of Jesse, a man after mine own heart, which shall fulfil all my will.

There were many others. There was Noah, who God used to save his family and every kind of animal from the flood that covered the whole earth. There was Elisha, who God used to perform amazing miracles. There was Esther, who God used to save the Jews from destruction. There was Mary, who God selected to be the mother of the Saviour of the world.

God knew all these people, and many more, who did wonderful things during their lives. Yet, God said that not one single one of them was greater than John the Baptist.

So, even though John never even did one miracle—not one—in the eyes of God, John was as important as all these other amazing people in the Bible.

John 10:41

41 And many resorted unto him, and said, John did no miracle: but all things that John spake of this man were true.

The question is, what made John great? He wasn't a king, and he didn't do any miracles. But God gave him the important task of preparing the way of the Lord Jesus Christ. His job was to make Jesus known.

If the most important things to John had been that his birth was announced by an angel, that his life was prophesied in the Old Testament, or that he was the cousin of Jesus, he would have been important in his own eyes, but he wouldn't have been great in God's eyes.

The most important thing to John was to make Jesus known. That's what made John great. He knew and followed God's purpose for his life. John was a humble man.

Proverbs 15:33

33 The fear of the LORD is the instruction of wisdom; and before honour is humility.

John recognized that the job God gave him—that of pointing people to Jesus—was the most important thing about him. When people would come to hear John's message, he would point them away from himself and to Jesus.

John 3:30

30 He must increase, but I must decrease.

TEACHER'S NOTE

humble —free from pride and arrogance; having a modest estimate of one's own worth; having a sense of one's own unworthiness in the sight of God and submission to His will.

John knew that any goodness in his life was a gift from God. And it's that way in our lives, too. Since God has given us the good things in our lives, He wants us to use those blessings.

John said about himself, "I'm just here to be a voice for Jesus, just like the prophets that were before me. We are all voices for Jesus. Get ready for Him."

John 1:23

23 He said, I am the voice of one crying in the wilderness, Make straight the way of the Lord, as said the prophet Esaias.

And that's what John was in his own eyes—just one voice. But he was one voice, and his voice made a difference. John recognized that his true value was in service for the Lord, doing what God made him to do; and he recognized that that made him very valuable.

It is the same with you. You are a voice for God. He designed you to make Him known to the world. You may have many blessings in your life, but the true value in your life is in service for the Lord—doing what God designed you to do—making Jesus known.

So, the question for you is, how can you make Jesus known?

- Like John the Baptist, humble yourself by submitting your heart to do God's will.

- Like John the Baptist, realize that the greatness in your life is that you belong to Jesus.

- Like John the Baptist, speak about the goodness of Jesus, rather than your own goodness.

- Like John the Baptist, choose to put Jesus first in your thoughts, words, and actions.

REVIEW GAME/QUESTIONS

Materials needed

Balloons

Push pins

Small containers with seals

Bag to hold containers

Set up

1. Blow up several balloons and arrange them into two stick figures of a man on the board or wall. There should be one balloon stick figure for each team.
2. Divide push pins into three separate small containers that are labeled with the numbers: 1, 2, 3.
3. Place the small labeled containers in a bag to conceal them.

Playing the Game

Ask a question to Team One. After a student answers correctly, allow him to come to the front, reach into the bag, and pick a container. The student can then pop the number of balloons that matches the number listed on the container. (So, if Container 3 is selected, the student can pop three balloons.) Alternate between Team One and Team Two. The first team to pop all their balloons wins.

Application

Sometimes it is easy for us to be filled with pride and prideful thoughts of ourselves. We should remember to get rid of any prideful thoughts. We should decrease, like John the Baptist (and like the man on the board!) so that Jesus can increase.

1. Where did John live until it was time for him to tell people Jesus was coming?
    Answer: In the wilderness

2. What were some of the things John ate when he lived in the wilderness? What did he wear?
    Answer: Wild honey and locusts; a robe of camels' hair tied with a leather belt.

3. Why were some of the Jewish leaders jealous of the coming Messiah John told them about?
    Answer: They were afraid that people would start following Jesus instead of them.

4. Why did some people think John was the Messiah?
    Answer: Because he knew so much about Jesus; because he baptized people

5. What did the voice from Heaven say when Jesus was baptized?
    Answer: "This is my beloved Son, in whom I am well pleased."

6. What did Jesus say about John?
    Answer: Of every person ever born, there was no one greater than John the Baptist.

7. Why didn't John mind it when people started following Jesus instead of him?
    Answer: He was humble.

8. What was the most important thing in life to John?
    Answer: Making Jesus known

9. What can we find our true value in?
    Answer: We find our true value in doing what God designed us to do.

10. What are you going to do today that will make Jesus known to others?
    Answer: Answers will vary.

Teaching the Memory Verse

John 3:30
30 He must increase, but I must decrease.

Materials Needed
Memory Verse Flashcards from the Ministry Resource download

Teaching the Verse
Repeat the verse together as a class several times. Each time, instruct the students to start reciting while on their tiptoes and shrink as they continue to recite the verse.

OBJECT LESSON
—Winning the Battle of Humility

Materials Needed

Boxing gloves

Lesson

Bring a pair of boxing gloves to class. (If you don't have access to a pair, an inexpensive pair of child's boxing gloves can often be purchased in a toy section of your local store.) Put the gloves on your hands or select a student who will wear the gloves as you teach the object lesson. Boxing gloves are used to show pride.

Application

Today, we are going to learn about humility! How many of you know what humility is? (Allow for feedback.) Humility is having a proper view of ourselves. It is thinking about ourselves less and about God and others more.

But living with humility is a constant struggle! It is way easier to think about what "I want" and what "I want to do." In addition to this, the world teaches us to be the best...to be bigger and better than everyone else.

But, Jesus teaches us to be humble. He wants us to decrease so He can increase!

Our spirit is always fighting between pride and humility. Sometimes, we will do something great, and we'll think very highly of ourselves. But, as soon as that happens, we should remember that we need to be humble. There is a constant battle between being prideful and being humble. After listening to today's lesson, it is my prayer that you will determine today to let humility win every time!

CRAFT—Pocket Pal

Supplies

Printables from the Ministry Resource download
Double sided tape
Magnet stickers

Instructions

1. Fold the John the Baptist cardstock just above the line.
2. Using double-sided tape, tape the right side and left side to make the pocket.
3. Add the magnet sticker to the back of the pocket chart.
4. Add the Bible verse.
5. Encourage the children to put the verse in order and to memorize it.

Application

We learned today that John the Baptist was a man of humility who constantly sought to lift up Jesus rather than himself. We should try to be just like John the Baptist who always talked about Jesus and who told others about Him rather than about himself.

ADDITIONAL RESOURCES

Find the following items on the Ministry Resource download:
- Coloring Page (for younger children)
- Activity Page (for older children)
- Student Take-Home Paper
- PowerPoint Presentation

Suggested Classroom Schedule

Before Class	Complete attendance record. Provide students with coloring pages/activity pages.
Opening	Welcome
Prayer	Prayer requests and praise reports from the children
Song Time	
Memory Verse	1 John 4:19
Song Time	
Object Lesson	God's Love
Bible Lesson	John
Application/Invitation	Help saved students apply lesson. Invite unsaved students to receive Christ.
Snack	Heart Shaped Cheese Pieces
Review Game/ Questions	
Craft	John and the Disciples Accordion
Closing	Give announcements and pray. Distribute take-home papers.

Lesson Two Overview

John
Theme—Love

Scripture
Mark 1:19–20 and John 19:26–27

Memory Verse
1 John 4:19 —*"We love him, because he first loved us."*

Lesson Outline
Introducing the Story
Our true story from the Bible today is about one of these disciples who learned something from walking with Jesus that he never could have learned any other way—true love.

Telling the Story
1. **Jesus Calls John** (*Matthew 4:21-22; Mark 1:19–20*)
   —*Flashcard 2.1*

2. **John Watches Jesus Perform Miracles**
   (*John 2, 4, 5, 6, 9, 11*)

3. **John Listens to Jesus** (*John 3, 4, 6, 8, 9, 10, 14*)
   —*Flashcard 2.2*

4. **John Cares for Jesus' Mother** (*John 19:26*)
   —*Flashcard 2.3*

Applying the Story
John didn't just follow Jesus' call to walk with Him. He listened to all Jesus said, and he let Jesus' words sink deep into his heart. John learned from following and walking with Jesus what true love looks like. He learned to love like Jesus loved.

LESSON TWO

John

Theme: Love

TEACHER'S CHECKLIST

- ❑ Read Mark 1:19–20 and John 19:26–27 daily.
- ❑ Study Lesson Two.
- ❑ Flash cards 2.1–2.3.
- ❑ Prepare snack—Heart-shaped cheese or fruit.
- ❑ Gather props for "Use an Object."
- ❑ Gather for object lesson—large foil pan, empty one-liter bottle, funnel, small glass, glass carafe, 1 packet of active dry yeast, 1 teaspoon clear liquid dish soap, ¼ cup water, 2 cups 40 volume clear hydrogen peroxide, red food coloring, carafe and liter labels from Ministry Resource download.
- ❑ Gather for game—packs of sticky notes (different colors) and small prizes for winners.
- ❑ Print for teaching the memory verse—"Heart Attack" hearts and Memory Verse Flashcards from the Ministry Resource download.
- ❑ Print for craft—Disciples printable from Ministry Resource download on white card stock.
- ❑ Print and duplicate Coloring Pages or Activity Pages on the Ministry Resource download (one per student).
- ❑ Print and duplicate the Take-Home Paper on the Ministry Resource download (one per student).

SCRIPTURES

Mark 1:19–20

19 And when he had gone a little further thence, he saw James the son of Zebedee, and John his brother, who also were in the ship mending their nets.

MEMORY VERSE

1 John 4:19
"We love him, because he first loved us."

20   And straightway he called them: and they left their father Zebedee in the ship with the hired servants, and went after him.

John 19:26–27

26   When Jesus therefore saw his mother, and the disciple standing by, whom he loved, he saith unto his mother, Woman, behold thy son!

27   Then saith he to the disciple, Behold thy mother! And from that hour that disciple took her unto his own home.

BIBLE LESSON

Introducing the Story

Have you ever wanted to learn how to do something, so you read a book to teach you how to do it? You can find books on just about any subject. You could read a book to teach you a craft, to teach you better grammar, or to teach you how to train a dog. Can you think of other things you could learn from books? (Allow students to answer.)

Or, you could take a class to learn something you are interested in. You could go to an art class to learn how to draw. The teacher would give you instructions and show you specific steps for drawing simple objects. Then, as you become good at the simple drawings, he or she would show you how to draw more complicated pictures.

The very first way we learn, when we are very small, is through being with and watching someone who knows more than we do. We watch our parents. We watch our older brothers and sisters. We watch everyone around us. As we watch, we also listen, and we follow what we see and hear. Do any of you have a little sister or brother? (Allow students to answer and to share specific incidents from their lives.) Then, you see this method of learning every day.

This is the way Jesus' twelve disciples learned to know and serve God. Jesus called them to come to Him and follow Him and watch what He did and listen to what He said.

While many people loved and followed Jesus, there were twelve men that Jesus chose especially to follow Him closely. Jesus had a special purpose for these men—He wanted them to teach others what He taught them.

These men were just regular people. There were Peter and Andrew—two brothers who were fishermen. Jesus told them that if they followed Him, He would make them fishers of men instead of fishers of fish! Then, there were

---

TEACHER'S TIP

When you as a teacher encourage your students to share specific life circumstances, you build their trust in your interest in them as individuals.

"People don't care how much you know until they know how much you care."
—Theodore Roosevelt

ACT IT OUT

Select twelve students to come to the front of the class and represent each of the disciples being mentioned.

---

two more fisher-man brothers—James and John, the sons of Zebedee. There was Philip, Nathanael (who was also called Bartholomew), and Thomas. There was Matthew, who was a tax collector. There was another James, the son of Alphaeus, and there was Lebbaeus. There was Simon the Canaanite; and, finally, there was Judas Iscariot, who later betrayed Jesus.

Matthew 10:2-4

2   Now the names of the twelve apostles are these; The first, Simon, who is called Peter, and Andrew his brother; James the son of Zebedee, and John his brother;

3   Philip, and Bartholomew; Thomas, and Matthew the publican; James the son of Alphaeus, and Lebbaeus, whose surname was Thaddaeus;

4   Simon the Canaanite, and Judas Iscariot, who also betrayed him.

These twelve men left their homes and followed Jesus wherever He went for three and a half years. They ate what Jesus ate. They slept where Jesus slept. They listened when Jesus taught. They watched Jesus pray. They watched Jesus heal sick people. They watched Jesus trust the Heavenly Father.

Our true story from the Bible today is about one of these disciples who learned something from walking with Jesus that he never could have learned any other way—true love.

Our story is about the disciple John.

The Story

1. Jesus Calls John (Matthew 4:21-22; Mark 1:19-20)

John grew up in a fishing family. His dad Zebedee was a fisherman—that's how he made money to provide for his family. Zebedee excelled at his job.

As a young boy, John probably loved fishing on the lake with his dad and his brother James. His father most likely taught him everything he knew about fishing. He taught him how to take care of the boats and nets and how to repair them when they needed it. He taught him how to know when the weather was right for fishing. He taught him the best spots to find fish and the best times of the day and night to catch fish.

As John grew older, fishing came naturally to him—after all, he had been doing it his whole life. And so, John went into business with his dad and his brother James.

> **USE AN OBJECT**
>
> You may also want to bring in props, such as fake or real fish, fishing poles, and coins or money for the disciples to hold as they stand before the class.

Flash Card 2.1 ➤

John worked hard and followed his father's instructions, because he knew his father was a successful fisherman who knew just what to do. One day, when the huge fishing net needed to be repaired, John and James sat in the boat at the side of the lake, mending the net.

"I love this business," John may have thought. "I can't quite explain—even to myself—the exhilarated feeling I get when I drag in this net full of fish. We put our all into it, and the success comes when we bring in a big catch."

He looked at James on the other side of the boat. "Aren't you glad Dad taught us everything he knows about fishing? We have a great future ahead of us."

The brothers heard a voice calling from the side of the lake, and they turned to see someone who had seen them long before they saw Him. "Follow me," the man called.

They recognized the man—they had met Jesus before. "It's Jesus, the Messiah—the Saviour we've been waiting for," the brothers said to each other. "Dad, the Messiah's calling us, and we need to follow Him," they said to Zebedee.

"Of course, follow the Messiah," their father said.

So, John and his brother James left all they knew and followed Jesus.

2. John Watches Jesus Perform Miracles (John 2, 4, 5, 6, 9, 11)

As John followed Jesus, walking with Him, talking with Him, eating with Him, and spending all his time with Him, he saw Jesus perform miracles.

- Jesus turned water into wine at a wedding feast (John 2:1–11).
- Jesus healed a rich man's son who was at the point of death (John 4:46–54).
- Jesus healed a man who had not been able to walk for thirty-eight years (John 5:1–17).
- Jesus turned five little loaves of bread and two small fish into enough food to feed over five thousand people (John 6:1–14).
- Jesus walked on top of the water over a stormy sea (John 6:15–21).
- Jesus gave sight to a man who had been blind since the time of his birth (John 9:1–41).
- Jesus raised His friend Lazarus from the dead after he had already been in the grave for four days (John 11:1–44).

When John saw the miracles, he realized that Jesus was doing what only God could do—he understood that Jesus is God.

TEACHER'S NOTE

miracle —an event or effect contrary to the established course of things; a deviation from the known laws of nature; a supernatural event, possible only through God's power

TEACHER'S NOTE

John saw Jesus perform many more miracles than these, but these are the miracles recorded in the book of John.

If time permits, you may want to more thoroughly describe one or more of these miracles.

John 20:30–31

30 And many other signs truly did Jesus in the presence of his disciples, which are not written in this book:

31 But these are written, that ye might believe that Jesus is the Christ, the Son of God; and that believing ye might have life through his name.

John understood something else. Jesus did all these things out of love. He saw the compassion in Jesus' eyes as Jesus looked into the face of the man who had been lame for thirty-eight years, with no hope of healing. He saw Jesus' love for the thousands of people who, with nothing to eat, had been listening to Jesus preach all day long, as He provided food for all of them. He understood Jesus' great love for His friends as He raised Lazarus from the dead. John understood that Jesus loved the people for whom He performed the miracles, and he understood that Jesus loved him.

1 John 4:8b

8 ...God is love.

And Jesus' love started changing John. As John spent time with Jesus, John started loving others like Jesus loved him.

1 John 4:11

11 Beloved, if God so loved us, we ought also to love one another.

3. John Listens to Jesus (John 3, 4, 6, 8, 9, 10, 14)

Flash Card 2.2

As John followed Jesus wherever He went, watching all the things Jesus did, and listening to Jesus' words, he heard Jesus preach many sermons, and he saw Him speak to many people.

- He heard Jesus tell Nicodemus that a person has to be born again to go to Heaven, and that God loves the whole world so much that He sent Jesus to die on the cross so that whoever believes in Jesus would be born again (John 3).

- He saw Jesus talk to a sinful woman at a well, and tell her that He could give her water for her spirit that would make her never thirst again (John 4).

TEACHER'S NOTE

If time permits, you may choose to more thoroughly describe one or more of these sermons or conversations.

- John heard Jesus preach that He was the bread of life. "He that cometh to me shall never hunger; and he that believeth on me shall never thirst," Jesus said (John 6:35).

- He was there when Jesus said, "I am the light of the world: he that followeth me shall not walk in darkness, but shall have the light of life" (John 8:12).

- John watched Jesus go to the blind man He had healed, and teach Him that salvation comes through believing in Jesus, after the religious rulers had cast the man out of the temple (John 9).

- John listened as Jesus shared that He is the Good Shepherd, who gives His life for His sheep (John 10).

- John heard Jesus comfort all the disciples, as He told them about the wonderful place He would prepare for them in Heaven (John 14).

John heard many more sermons, and listened to Jesus speak to many more people, and each time, John understood more and more that Jesus loved every person, and Jesus loved John.

"He loves me—Jesus loves me more than I can imagine!" John thought. "And His love makes me love Him more and more each day."

1 John 4:19

19 We love him, because he first loved us.

In the book of John (one of the five books of the Bible written by John), we see that John felt so loved by Jesus that he called himself "the disciple whom Jesus loved." (It seems that sometimes John felt like Jesus loved him more than anyone else in the world!)

God used John to write one of the most well-known verses in the Bible— one that tells about the greatest love that has ever been shown—John 3:16.

John 3:16

16 For God so loved the world, that he gave his only begotten Son, that whosoever believeth in him should not perish, but have everlasting life.

4. John Cares for Jesus' Mother (John 19:26)

From following Jesus—from walking with Him, listening to Him, asking Him questions, eating with Him, and watching Him, John realized that the more he

---

TEACHER'S NOTE

You may wish to share the names of the five books penned by John:

After Jesus was crucified and had risen again from the dead, and after John had lived many more years and had become an older man, God used John to write five books of the New Testament. Does anyone think you know the name of at least one of those books? (Allow students to answer.) He wrote John, first, second, and third John, and Revelation.

---

knew Jesus, the more he wanted to know Jesus. And the more he knew Jesus, the more he knew that Jesus loved him. And the more he knew that Jesus loved him, the more he loved Jesus.

John didn't just know that Jesus loved him—he believed it with his whole heart. He believed the truth that Jesus loved him so much that He wanted him to be part of His family—His own child!

John 1:12

12 But as many as received him, to them gave he power to become the sons of God, even to them that believe on his name:

"Jesus loves me," thought John, as with a broken heart he stood by while Jesus hung on the cross to pay for John's sins and the sins of everyone else in the whole world.

Then Jesus spoke to His mother Mary, who was standing near John at the foot of the cross. "Mother, look at John. He is going to take care of you as if you were his own mother."

Then Jesus turned his eyes to John and said, "Care for her as if she were your own mother."

> **Flash Card 2.3**

John 19:26–27

26 When Jesus therefore saw his mother, and the disciple standing by, whom he loved, he saith unto his mother, Woman, behold thy son!

27 Then saith he to the disciple, Behold thy mother! And from that hour that disciple took her unto his own home.

Jesus' love had been growing in John's heart so much all along as he had followed Jesus, that he already loved Mary like she was his own mother. After all, John had become part of Jesus' family when he trusted Him as his Saviour from sin. John took Mary to his own home and cared for her as if she was his own mother.

"I can hardly believe God's love," John wrote years later. "He loves me so much that He sent Jesus to pay for my sins so I could become His child. I am in His family, and He has even given me His name. Now, that's love!"

1 John 3:1a

1 Behold, what manner of love the Father hath bestowed upon us, that we should be called the sons of God.

APPLYING THE STORY

John referred to himself as "the disciple whom Jesus loved" (John 13:23, 19:26, 20:2, 21:7, 21:20). Did Jesus love all His disciples, or did He just love John? (Allow students to share thoughts.)

God's Word says that God loves everybody and that no one is more important to Him than anyone else.

1 John 4:16

16 And we have known and believed the love that God hath to us. God is love; and he that dwelleth in love dwelleth in God, and God in him.

Romans 2:11

11 For there is no respect of persons with God.

Acts 10:34

34 Then Peter opened his mouth, and said, Of a truth I perceive that God is no respecter of persons.

Some people, like John, feel more loved by God than others feel. Those are the people who let God's love change them.

John didn't just follow Jesus' call to walk with Him, he got as close to Jesus as he could. He listened to all Jesus said, and he let Jesus' words sink deep into his heart. He learned to love like Jesus loved.

John learned from following and walking with Jesus what true love looks like. More than just a feeling, true love shows in a person's life. Love for God causes us to want to obey Him.

John 14:15

15 If ye love me, keep my commandments.

When we obey God out of love for Him, we have a desire to know what His commandments are. "The greatest commandment," Jesus said, "is to love God with all your heart, soul, and mind."

Matthew 22:37–38

37 Jesus said unto him, Thou shalt love the Lord thy God with all thy heart, and with all thy soul, and with all thy mind.

38 This is the first and great commandment.

Matthew 22:39

39 And the second is like unto it, Thou shalt love thy neighbour as thyself.

John 15:12

12 This is my commandment, That ye love one another, as I have loved you.

1 John 4:21

21 And this commandment have we from him, That he who loveth God love his brother also.

Do you love God with all your heart, soul, and mind? Do you love your neighbors, which means, do you love others?

The way you can test your love for God and others is to look at your life:

- Do you spend time with God—reading His Word and talking to Him?
- Do you often think about how much He loves you?
- Do you ask Him to change you through His love and through His Word?
- Does knowing that He loves you make you think, "It's so amazing that God loves me! I know I don't deserve His love, but it makes me love Him right back."
- Does His love make you love others enough to share His love with them through sharing the gospel?
- Does it make you love others enough to put their needs and/or desires ahead of your own?

When God's love changes us, we love others with the love He has given us.

REVIEW GAME/QUESTIONS

Materials needed
Packs of sticky notes
Small prizes for winners

Set Up
Divide your class into groups (at least two), each group being led by a class assistant or worker. Assign a certain color of sticky notes to each team, and hand the worker the pack of notes.

Playing the Game
Instruct the students to work together within groups to come up with as many questions as possible in which the answer to the question is, "John." For

example: "Who is the disciple whom Jesus loved?" "Who wrote John 3:16?" "Who wrote five books in the Bible?"

As the students generate questions, your class assistants will write them on the sticky notes. When you have determined that sufficient time has passed, end this portion of the game and ask the workers to place their team's sticky notes on the board. The team with the most sticky notes wins.

Take time to review the questions written by the students to reinforce the lesson. Then, continue with the questions below, rewarding individual students with a small prize for answering the following questions:

1. What is the method by which we first learn?
   Answer: By being with and watching someone who knows more than we do.

2. What was John's father's job?
   Answer: He was a fisherman.

3. Who was the Man who called to James and John while they were fishing?
   Answer: Jesus

4. What were some of the miracles John saw Jesus perform?
   Answer: Answers will vary, but should include miracles from Point 2.

5. What motivated Jesus to perform all these miracles for people?
   Answer: Love

6. By what name did John refer to himself in the book of John?
   Answer: "The disciple whom Jesus loved."

7. What is one of the most well-known verses in the Bible—one that God used John to write?
   Answer: John 3:16

8. While Jesus was on the cross, who did He tell John to take care of?
   Answer: Jesus' mother, Mary

9. Why do some people feel more like God loves them than other people do?
   Answer: Because they spend time with Him and let God's love change them.

10. What did Jesus say are the two greatest commandments?
    Answer: 1. Love the Lord with all your heart, soul, and mind. 2. Love your neighbor as yourself.

Teaching the Memory Verse

1 John 4:19

19   We love him, because he first loved us.

Materials Needed

"Heart Attack" hearts from the Ministry Resource download

Memory Verse Flashcards from the Ministry Resource download

Set Up

Print and cut out the "Heart Attack" hearts from the Ministry Resource download (containing one word from the verse on each card).

Make two sets—one for each team.

Tape the hearts all over the classroom (on the walls, board, desks, etc).

Teaching the Verse

Say the verse together as a class several times. Once the students are familiar with the verse, divide the class into two teams. When you say, "Go," the teams can race to collect each word in the verse and arrange in the pocket chart (or dry-erase board ledge) at the front of the class. The first team to put the verse in the correct order wins.

OBJECT LESSON—God's Love

Materials Needed

Large foil pan

Empty one-liter bottle

Funnel

Small glass

Glass carafe

1 packet of Active Dry Yeast

1 teaspoon clear liquid dish soap

¼ cup water

2 cups 40 Volume Clear Hydrogen Peroxide (can be purchased at beauty supply store or on amazon.com)

Red food coloring (approximately 15 drops)

Carafe and Liter Labels from Ministry Resource download

Set up

Attach the "God's Love" adhesive label to the glass carafe, and attach the "YOU" adhesive label to the empty one-liter bottle. Pour the hydrogen peroxide and red food coloring into the glass carafe. Pour the clear liquid dish wash soap into the empty one-liter bottle. Pour the packet of yeast into the small juice glass. Place the one-liter bottle inside the large foil pan. Set the carafe and juice glass to the side.

Lesson

"Aren't you just so thankful for God's love?! Jesus' love can fill our hearts with gratitude and love for Him and others, if we will let it.

Let's say this plastic bottle represents you. And, this beautiful glass of red liquid represents God's love for you. (The color red reminds us of love. It also reminds us of the blood Jesus shed on the cross.)"

Ask your students to give examples of the ways God expresses their love to them. Examples may include that He died on the cross for us, that He will always be with us, etc. Each time an example is given, pour a little bit of the peroxide mixture into the water bottle. Do this 3–4 times (following 3–4 examples of God's love).

"God's love for us is so wonderful! The Bible says that His love for us is what causes our hearts to love Him and others. Our verse for today reminds us of this truth:

> **1 John 4:19**
>
> 19　We love him, because he first loved us.

If you don't feel very loving toward others or even toward God, you can ask Him to help you show His love. I have another small glass here. This glass contains active yeast. Do you know what yeast does? It helps things to GROW! So this glass of yeast will represent prayer. As we pray and spend time with God, like the Apostle John did in today's story, our love for Him and for others will grow!"

As you say the next sentence, pour the yeast into the one-liter bottle that now contains the red hydrogen peroxide and liquid dish wash soap mixture. As soon as you add the yeast, the contents of the bottle will overflow (perhaps for up to a minute or two).

"As I spend time reading my Bible, praying, and studying God's Word, His amazing love for me becomes overwhelming, and I can't help but explode with love for Him and the people around me. And, as I continue spending time with God, His love continues to flow through me."

Application

"This week, take the time to be with Jesus. Talk to Him. Spend time with Him. Thank Him for loving you so much! And then, as you grow in your thankfulness for His love, let it flow through you to the friends and family God has placed in your life."

Consider concluding this object lesson by asking for examples of more ways God shows His love to us, and ways that the students can demonstrate God's love to others throughout the week.

CRAFT—John and the Disciples Accordion

Supplies

Disciples printable from Ministry Resource download
White card stock

Instructions

1. Print page 1 and page 2 of the disciples printable on one sheet of white card stock.
2. Cut into 3 strips so that there are 12 disciples on one side of the card stock and facts about the disciples on the back side.
3. Give one disciples printable to each student.
4. Instruct each student to fold the disciples printable back and forth making an accordion.

Application

Once the students are done, play a trivia game using the facts about the disciples.

ADDITIONAL RESOURCES

Find the following items on the Ministry Resource download:

- Coloring Page (for younger children)
- Activity Page (for older children)
- Student Take-Home Paper
- PowerPoint Presentation

Suggested Classroom Schedule

Before Class	Complete attendance record. Provide students with coloring pages/activity pages.	
Opening	Welcome	
Prayer	Prayer requests and praise reports from the children	
Song Time		
Memory Verse	Psalm 95:6	
Song Time		
Object Lesson	Doing What Is Needful	
Bible Lesson	Mary and Martha	
Application/Invitation	Help saved students apply lesson. Invite unsaved students to receive Christ.	
Snack	"M&M" Cookies	
Review Game/ Questions		
Craft	Mary & Martha Mini Notepad	
Closing	Give announcements and pray. Distribute take-home papers.	

Lesson Three Overview

Mary and Martha
Theme—Devotion

Scripture
Luke 10:38–42

Memory Verse
Psalm 95:6 — *"O come, let us worship and bow down: let us kneel before the LORD our maker."*

Lesson Outline
Introducing the Story
Would you believe that Jesus had favorite places to stay when He lived on this earth? In our true story from the Bible, we will learn what makes a home special to Jesus.

Telling the Story
1. **Martha Receives Jesus into Their Home**
   (Luke 10:38)—Flashcard 3.1

2. **Mary Spends Time with Jesus**
   (Luke 10:39)—Flashcard 3.2

3. **Martha Gets Upset** *(Luke 10:40)—Flashcard 3.3*

4. **Jesus Answers.** *(Luke 10:41–42)*

Applying the Story
When we spend time with Jesus, He gives us peace in place of stress, trust in place of worry, and gladness and kindness in place of anger. What a great way to serve Him!

LESSON THREE
Mary and Martha
Theme: Devotion

TEACHER'S CHECKLIST

- ☐ Read Luke 10:38–42.
- ☐ Study Lesson Three.
- ☐ Flash cards 3.1–3.3.
- ☐ Prepare snack—"M&M" Cookies.
- ☐ Gather objects for "Use an Object."
- ☐ Gather for object lesson—jar, ping pong balls, rice.
- ☐ Gather for review game— M&M game pieces from the Ministry Resource download, poster board, marker, blindfold, M&M candies.
- ☐ Gather **for teaching the memory verse**—Memory Verse Flashcards from the Ministry Resource download, worshipful music, and a music player.
- ☐ Gather for craft—address mailing labels, Mary & Martha printable template from Ministry Resource download, mini notepads.
- ☐ Print for review game—M&M game pieces from the Ministry Resource download.
- ☐ Print Memory Verse Flashcards from the Ministry Resource download.
- ☐ Print for craft—Mary & Martha printable template from Ministry Resource download.
- ☐ Print and duplicate Coloring Pages or Activity Pages on the Ministry Resource download (one per student).
- ☐ Print and duplicate the Take-Home Paper on the Ministry Resource download (one per student).

SCRIPTURES

Luke 10:38–42

38 Now it came to pass, as they went, that he entered into a certain village: and a certain woman named Martha received him into her house.

39 And she had a sister called Mary, which also sat at Jesus' feet, and heard his word.

MEMORY VERSE

Psalm 95:6
"O come, let us worship and bow down: let us kneel before the LORD our maker."

40   But Martha was cumbered about much serving, and came to him, and said, Lord, dost thou not care that my sister hath left me to serve alone? bid her therefore that she help me.

41   And Jesus answered and said unto her, Martha, Martha, thou art careful and troubled about many things:

42   But one thing is needful: and Mary hath chosen that good part, which shall not be taken away from her.

USE AN OBJECT

Bring a bag to class full of various items that we enjoy using (sometimes even to serve others), but don't absolutely need. These items could include: an iPad, a large candy bar, children's books, kitchen items (to help your mom), garden tools (to help a grandparent plant a garden), etc. Also include a Bible in your bag.

Take time to talk about each item as you or a student pulls it out of your bag. Once they have all been removed and discussed, ask your students, "Are any of these items bad? No! But, of all the items in this bag, which one is the most needful? Of course! Spending time with God in His Word is the most important thing we can do every day."

BIBLE LESSON

Introducing the Story

If you could choose anyone's home in the whole world to spend time in, whose home would you choose? (Allow students to answer, and encourage them to share why they would choose the specific home they mention.)

We generally like to be where we feel cared about and comfortable. We like to be with people whom we know love us.

What are some things that make you cared for by someone? (Encourage answers.)

- We feel cared about when someone's eyes light up when they see us.

- We may feel cared about by someone who says kind and encouraging things and speaks in a gentle tone of voice.

- We may feel cared about because someone has special treats at their house for us, letting us know they thought about us and were glad we were coming to see them.

- We may feel cared about when someone drops everything they are doing to spend time with us.

We really wouldn't choose to spend time at someone's house who ignores us (although we may have to spend time with people like this sometimes). We wouldn't choose to be with someone who yells at us or is unkind to us in any way.

Would you believe that Jesus had favorite places to stay when He lived on this earth? In our true story from the Bible, we will learn what makes a home special to Jesus.

The Story

1. Martha Receives Jesus into Their Home. (Luke 10:38)

In the town of Bethany, about two miles east of Jerusalem, lived two sisters—Martha and Mary—and their brother, Lazarus. These sisters and brother were such special friends of Jesus' that God made sure to tell us specifically that Jesus loved them, even though we already know He loves everybody.

John 11:5

5   Now Jesus loved Martha, and her sister, and Lazarus.

When Jesus went to Bethany, theirs was the home He chose to visit. And, Jesus didn't just like to visit them; they liked to have Jesus visit. When Jesus came to town, Martha welcomed Him into their home.

Luke 10:38

38   Now it came to pass, as they went, that he entered into a certain village: and a certain woman named Martha received him into her house.

Now, when Martha welcomed Jesus into their home, she didn't just point to a chair and say, "Have a seat," and go on with her business.

Jesus' visits were big events to Martha. She loved Jesus, and she wanted everything to be perfect for Him. She cleaned the house, prepared a special meal, and used the nicest dishes. "Only the best for Jesus," Martha thought as she made everything ready.

It was a lot of work in Martha's day to prepare a meal. They didn't have refrigerators, as we do now, so all their food had to be prepared fresh every day. If they wanted milk, they had to milk the cow or goat. If they wanted meat, they had to kill a sheep or cow. If they wanted fruit or vegetables, they had to pick them from the garden or purchase them at the market. And, they didn't have stoves like we do. They cooked over a stone or clay oven, usually in a kitchen that was a separate building from the rest of the house, so the house wouldn't fill with smoke or become too hot during meal preparation.

So, when Martha prepared for Jesus, it was a sacrifice of her time and energy to make everything special for Him.

TEACHER'S NOTE

You will want to be sensitive to emotional responses from students. If a student shares that he or she does not feel cared for, this would be a great circumstance to gently offer to talk with them after class, using the opportunity to share God's grace as "a very present help in trouble" (Psalm 46:1).

Flash Card 3.1

2. Mary Spends Time with Jesus. (Luke 10:39)

Luke 10:39

39   And she had a sister called Mary, which also sat at Jesus' feet, and heard his word.

Flash Card 3.2 ➤

Jesus' visits to their home were big events to Mary, too. Mary likely did her best to always have the house clean and ready for company. She probably made sure they had simple foods ready to serve so they could welcome guests at any time.

Then, when Jesus was actually at their house, Mary felt like everything was ready, and she could spend time with Him, which was her favorite thing to do. Jesus would sit down in a chair, and Mary would sit on the floor at His feet, honoring Him and listening to every word He spoke. Mary loved Jesus' words and wanted to be with Him more than anything in the whole world. Mary was devoted to Jesus.

Psalm 95:6

6   O come, let us worship and bow down: let us kneel before the LORD our maker.

Psalm 119:97; 103

97   O how love I thy law! it is my meditation all the day.

103 How sweet are thy words unto my taste! yea, sweeter than honey to my mouth!

3. Martha Gets Upset. (Luke 10:40)

Luke 10:40

40   But Martha was cumbered about much serving, and came to him, and said, Lord, dost thou not care that my sister hath left me to serve alone? bid her therefore that she help me.

Martha didn't feel like everything was ready for Jesus. She didn't want to give Jesus just a simple meal—He was special, and she wanted it to be perfect. While Mary sat listening at Jesus' feet, Martha, who was working in the kitchen, was getting angrier by the minute.

"Why doesn't she help me?" Martha said to herself. "Can't she see there's so much to do? And there she sits, having a good time with Jesus while I do all the work!"

Flash Card 3.3 ➤

Poor Martha! She wasn't feeling very devoted to Jesus at that moment. She wasn't thinking about Jesus' words being sweeter than honey and how much she loved them. She wasn't thinking about kneeling before Him.

Instead of thinking about the special relationship Jesus wanted to build with her, Martha was thinking about all the special things she wanted to do for Him.

Finally, she just couldn't take it anymore. Martha marched straight into the room where Jesus and Mary sat talking. "Jesus," she demanded, "don't you care that Mary just sits there, leaving me to do all the work by myself? Tell her to come and help me!"

4. Jesus Answers. (Luke 10:41–42)

Luke 10:41–42

41   And Jesus answered and said unto her, Martha, Martha, thou art careful and troubled about many things:

42   But one thing is needful: and Mary hath chosen that good part, which shall not be taken away from her.

Jesus, who knows everything, understood exactly what Martha was going through in her heart. He knew she wanted to honor Him by making a very special meal, but He also knew her heart was not honoring Him in the work she was doing. Her heart was worried (careful), stressed (troubled), and she didn't have peace.

Philippians 4:6

6   Be careful for nothing; but in every thing by prayer and supplication with thanksgiving let your requests be made known unto God.

Jesus knew that doing things for Him was more important to Martha at that moment than spending time with Him. He wanted Martha to know the peace that comes through just sitting at His feet, like Mary was doing.

Philippians 4:7

7   And the peace of God, which passeth all understanding, shall keep your hearts and minds through Christ Jesus.

Jesus looked kindly into Martha's eyes. "Martha, Martha," He said, "thou art careful and troubled about many things: But one thing is needful: and Mary hath chosen that good part, which shall not be taken away from her."

Jesus wanted Martha to understand, "We don't need a lot of things. We could get by with just a simple meal. We don't need special dishes or a beautiful flower arrangement on the table. Those things are nice, but they last only a short while.

"If those things cause your heart to be troubled, they aren't the best things for you. Even though they seem like good things—things you want to do for me—when you do them with an angry or troubled spirit, they actually draw you away from me, rather than close to me. I know that's not what you want.

"Mary has chosen the good part—that which won't be taken away from her. All the other things we do come and go, but My Word and My love will never pass away. I want you to choose the good part, too."

John 6:63b

63 ...the words that I speak unto you, they are spirit, and they are life.

Matthew 24:35

35 Heaven and earth shall pass away, but my words shall not pass away.

Romans 8:35–39

35 Who shall separate us from the love of Christ? shall tribulation, or distress, or persecution, or famine, or nakedness, or peril, or sword?

36 As it is written, For thy sake we are killed all the day long; we are accounted as sheep for the slaughter.

37 Nay, in all these things we are more than conquerors through him that loved us.

38 For I am persuaded, that neither death, nor life, nor angels, nor principalities, nor powers, nor things present, nor things to come,

39 Nor height, nor depth, nor any other creature, shall be able to separate us from the love of God, which is in Christ Jesus our Lord.

Applying the Story

Mary and Martha both loved the Lord. We know Mary was doing exactly what the Lord wanted her to do, because Jesus said so.

When Martha told Jesus to direct Mary to help her, Jesus didn't follow Martha's instructions. Instead, He told her that Mary had chosen the needful—the most important—thing.

But, was Martha doing something wrong? Wasn't she trying to serve the Lord? (Allow students to respond.) What was she doing to serve Him? (Allow students to respond.) She was going all out to make a special meal. She wanted everything just right. Those were good things to do.

But, Martha was also stressing and worrying and fussing over all the details. And she was getting mad that Mary was sitting at Jesus' feet instead of helping her. Those were not good things.

Shouldn't we serve the Lord? Yes, God's Word tells us to serve Him—with gladness.

Psalm 100:2a

2   Serve the LORD with gladness...

When we lose the gladness in our serving, we can know that it's time for us to just sit at Jesus' feet, spending time with Him, worshiping Him, and listening to Him through His Word. Those emotions of worry, stress, fussing, and anger can serve as yellow "caution" lights, reminding us we need to get our focus back on spending time with the Lord so we can gladly do things for the Lord.

That's what devotions are all about—spending time with the Lord, building our relationship with Him. When our relationship with Him is strong, He gives us peace in place of stress, trust in place of worry, and gladness and kindness in place of anger. What a great way to serve Him.

Do you have devotions—time set aside in your heart and in your day—to spend only with the Lord?

- Do you schedule your day so you can be with Him?

- Do you sit at His feet, listening to His words through the Bible?

- Do you share your heart and your burdens with Him?

- Do you tell Him how much you love Him?

- Do you thank Him for His goodness to you?

It's so easy for us to allow other things to take the place of the "good part"—the part that Mary chose. Let's tell the Lord we are going to purpose to choose "that good part"—spending time with Him.

TEACHER'S NOTE

This would be a wonderful opportunity for you to share with your students how you spend your devotional time—your quiet time with the Lord.

You may wish to print up a simple sheet with a list of ideas for devotions. It could be a simple as:

1. Tell God you love Him.
2. Ask Him to teach you as you read His Word.
3. Read 1 chapter.
4. Pray.
   - Praise Him.
   - Ask Him for forgiveness for sins you have committed that day.
   - Ask Him for wisdom.
   - Pray for people you love.
5. Write down a verse to memorize.

REVIEW GAME/QUESTIONS

Materials needed

M&M game pieces from the Ministry Resource download

Poster board

Marker

Blindfold

M&M's or small candy

Set Up

On the poster board, draw nine large squares. You can decorate the edges of your board with M&M candy décor (such as wrappers or a bulletin board border). Place an M&M game piece in each square. The poster board can be placed flat on a table or secured on the chalkboard with game pieces attached to the squares with velcro.

Playing the Game

Ask review questions from the list below. When a student answers correctly, your class assistant or helper will put a blindfold over their eyes. When the student is unable to see, the other classmates will work together to select a "Secret Square." Once the square has been selected, the student can remove the blindfold and begin removing M&M pieces from the squares. When the student selects the M&M piece from the Secret Square, the rest of the class yells, "STOP!" At that point, the student stops selecting squares and receives a piece of candy for every M&M selected before getting to the Secret Square. If the student was able to remove 3 M&M game pieces before choosing one from the Secret Square, he can receive small pieces of candy as his reward for answering the question.

Ask a class assistant to reset the game pieces while you ask the next question. The process is repeated until each student has a turn or until all the questions have been asked.

1.   What were the names of the two sisters Jesus liked to spend time with?
     Answer: Martha and Mary

2.   What town did they live in?
     Answer: Bethany, about 2 miles from Jerusalem

3.   What did Martha like to do when Jesus came to visit?
     Answer: She liked to prepare special meals and things for Him.

4.   What did Mary like to do when Jesus came to visit?
     Answer: She liked to sit at His feet and listen to Him.

5. What did Martha do when Mary didn't help her serve the meal?
    Answer: She got angry and told Jesus He should tell Mary to help her.

6. How did Jesus already know that Martha was troubled?
    Answer: Jesus knows everything.

7. What was the "good part" Jesus said Mary had chosen?
    Answer: Spending time with Jesus, listening to His words.

8. How long will God's words last?
    Answer: Forever

9. Was Martha doing right or wrong to serve the Lord?
    Answer: She was doing right to serve Him, but she was doing wrong to become worried, upset, and angry as she did it.

10. What are some things you have allowed in your life that take the place of "that good part" in your life? What will you do this week to make sure you spend time with the Lord?
    Answer: Answers will vary.

Teaching the Memory Verse

Psalm 95:6

6   O come, let us worship and bow down: let us kneel before the LORD our maker.

Materials Needed
Memory Verse Flashcards from Ministry Resource download
Worshipful music
A music player (such as your smartphone or CD player)

Teaching the Verse
Recite the verse as a class several times, using the Memory Verse Flashcards. When you feel the students have learned the verse, you can play a modified version of musical chairs. Arrange the chairs in a manner conducive for this game (making sure there is one less chair for the number of students in your class) and consider playing songs that specifically mention worshipping the Lord or being devoted to Him.

Play the music as the students walk around the chairs. When the music stops, the student who does not have a chair is not "out," but rather, gets to say the verse from memory.

Play another round, but do not remove a chair each time. All the students can continue playing, and each time, the student who is without a chair when the music stops, recites the verse from memory.

If a student has trouble recalling the verse, the entire class can help by reciting it together before playing again.

OBJECT LESSON
—Doing What Is Needful

Materials Needed

Jar
3 ping pong balls
Rice

Lesson

Set the items listed above on a table or desk, and tell your students what each item represents. The jar represents our lives. The rice represents a lot of things we like to do that fill up our lives. (Ask students for examples of what they enjoy doing with their time—riding our bikes, playing with friends, playing a computer game, watching a movie, etc.)The ping pong balls represent the needful and important things we should do in our lives. These things would include reading the Bible, praying, and going to church to hear His Word.

Fill the jar with the rice, and as you pour it in, say something similar to, "It is so easy to fill up our lives with all the fun things we like to do! It's so easy to play with our friends, or sleep in really late, or play with legos and dolls." Now, try to fit the ping pong balls in the jar. As you do this, tell your students, "If we fill up our lives with all those fun activities, sadly, we won't have time for the most important and needful things in our lives. If we play so hard all day, we may be too tired to pray at night. If we sleep in late, we might not have time to read our Bible before we go to school. If we choose to play sports on a Sunday, this would keep us from going to church to learn more about God."

Next, separate the rice and ping pong balls back into their original containers, and explain, "But, it is so cool to know that if we do what God tells us is most needful first, then we will have time to fit in all the other things that we want to do!"

Place the ping pong balls in the jar first this time, and re-iterate what these balls represent. Proceed with pouring the rice in the jar, demonstrating that all the rice fit if we put the most important things in first. (**Note:** Before class, be sure to measure the right proportion of rice to use with the ping pong balls and jars.)

Application

God praised Mary for doing what was needful. Did she help Martha clean and serve? Yes! But, she kept her priorities right by still sitting at the feet of Jesus when He was at their house. This week, strive to do those needful things first, then watch how God will allow you to do other activities you want to accomplish, as well.

CRAFT—Mary & Martha Mini Notepad

Supplies

Address mailing labels
Mary & Martha printables from Ministry Resource download
Mini notepads—one per student (If available, use a heart shaped notepad.)

Instructions

1. Print the Mary & Martha labels.
2. Give each student one mini notepad and one of each label (there are two).
3. Instruct the students to put one label on the front of the mini note pad and the other label on the back.

Application

Encourage the students to write down their favorite Bible verses in the note pad and think about them throughout the week.

ADDITIONAL RESOURCES

Find the following items on the Ministry Resource download:

- Coloring Page (for younger children)
- Activity Page (for older children)
- Student Take-Home Paper
- PowerPoint Presentation

Suggested Classroom Schedule

Before Class	Complete attendance record. Provide students with coloring pages/activity pages.
Opening	Welcome
Prayer	Prayer requests and praise reports from the children
Song Time	
Memory Verse	2 Corinthians 5:17
Song Time	
Object Lesson	Beautiful Transformations
Bible Lesson	Mary Magdalene
Application/Invitation	Help saved students apply lesson. Invite unsaved students to receive Christ.
Snack	Butterfly Snack Bags
Review Game/ Questions	
Craft	Mary Magdalene Transition Ink Pen
Closing	Give announcements and pray. Distribute take-home papers.

Lesson Four Overview

Mary Magdalene
Theme—Transformation

Scripture
Luke 8:1-3

Memory Verse
2 Corinthians 5:17— *"Therefore if any man be in Christ, he is a new creature: old things are passed away; behold, all things are become new."*

Lesson Outline
Introducing the Story
God gave us a world full of change as kind of "pictures" to help us understand what He does in us. When we allow God to work in our lives, He changes our hearts and lives so we become very different than we were before Jesus came in.

Telling the Story
1. **Mary Magdalene's Life Before She Met Jesus**
   (Luke 8:1-3)—Flashcard 4.1
2. **Mary Magdalene Meets Jesus**
   (Luke 8:2; Mark 16:9)
3. **Mary Magdalene's New Life** *(Luke 8:3)*
   —Flashcard 4.2
4. **Mary's New Life Continues** *(Mark 15:40–41)*
   —Flashcard 4.3

Applying the Story
Salvation is a life transformation. It makes us a new "creation" in Christ. We were under the curse of the penalty of sin, but we are now free from that curse. We no longer serve Satan—we are free to serve Jesus Christ.

LESSON FOUR
4 Mary Magdalene
Theme: Transformation

TEACHER'S CHECKLIST

- ☐ Read Matthew 27:55–56, 28; Mark 15:40–41; 16; Luke 8:1–3; 23:55–24:12; John 19:25; 20:1–18.
- ☐ Study Lesson Four.
- ☐ Flash cards 4.1–4.3.
- ☐ Prepare snack—Butterfly Snack Bags.
- ☐ Gather for review game—scissors, white cardstock, Crayola Color Switchers markers.
- ☐ Gather for object lesson—pitcher of water, ice cube trays.
- ☐ Gather for craft—Mary Magdalene printable from the Ministry Resource download, retractable ink pens (one per student), craft glue or double-sided tape.
- ☐ Print for craft—Mary Magdalene printable from the Ministry Resource download.
- ☐ Print Memory Verse Flashcards from the Ministry Resource download.
- ☐ Print and duplicate Coloring Pages or Activity Pages on the Ministry Resource download (one per student).
- ☐ Print and duplicate Take-Home Paper on the Ministry Resource download (one per student).

SCRIPTURES

Luke 8:1–3

1 And it came to pass afterward, that he went throughout every city and village, preaching and shewing the glad tidings of the kingdom of God: and the twelve were with him,

2 And certain women, which had been healed of evil spirits and infirmities, Mary called Magdalene, out of whom went seven devils,

SNACK SUGGESTION

Butterfly Snack Bags
Fill snack-sized Ziploc bags with a small snack of your choice (such as goldfish, raisins, cheerios, or a small assortment of the combined items). Leave enough room in the bag to create a space in the middle of the bag. In that space, clip a clothespin. The clothespin is the body of the butterfly. Decorate (or allow the students to decorate) the clothespin and attach chenille wire to the top to serve as the antennas.

MEMORY VERSE

2 Corinthians 5:17
"Therefore if any man be in Christ, he is a new creature: old things are passed away; behold, all things are become new."

3 And Joanna the wife of Chuza Herod's steward, and Susanna, and many others, which ministered unto him of their substance.

BIBLE LESSON

Introducing the Story

We live in a world full of change.

We change. We are first born into this world as little babies who can do nothing for ourselves. Then we slowly grow, continually changing throughout our lives.

Our seasons change. We have cold winter, when the trees are bare and the grass is dead. Then spring comes, and everything begins to look alive again. We have summer, when the flowers are blooming, and everything is bright and green. Then comes fall, when the leaves change color and eventually die and fall from the trees. And then we're back to winter.

Some things change forms. When water freezes, it becomes ice, and when ice melts, it becomes water. When we heat water to a high enough temperature, it becomes steam.

Animals change. We see great change in the life of a butterfly. The butterfly doesn't start out beautiful and free, gliding through the air. He is first a caterpillar—a worm-like little creature. He spends this short time of his life doing little more than eating. Finally, when the time is right, the caterpillar spins a cocoon, or chrysalis; and that chrysalis becomes its "bed" where it sleeps for several weeks. Inside the chrysalis, the caterpillar changes, and again, when the time is right, he sheds the chrysalis and comes out transformed—a beautiful butterfly.

God gave us a world full of change as kind of "pictures" to help us understand what He does in us. When we allow God to work in our lives, He changes our hearts and lives so we become very different than we were before Jesus came in.

Another word for change is *transformation*, and today we are going to study a woman in the New Testament whose life was transformed by the Lord Jesus Christ.

The Story

1. Mary Magdalene's Life Before She Met Jesus (Luke 8:1–3)

As Jesus traveled, teaching and preaching, He often healed people. Can anyone think of diseases and other physical problems Jesus healed while He was on Earth?

(Allow students to respond.) He gave sight to blind people. He healed people of the disease of leprosy. He healed paralyzed and lame people. He healed people with all kinds of diseases, and He even gave life again to some people who had died.

Jesus went to many small villages and towns throughout Israel. In one of the villages He met a woman who was in great need of healing. Her sickness wasn't one you could see—not a broken leg, or sores covering her body, or blindness.

Her problem was on the inside, and it made her life absolutely miserable.

Mary Magdalene was possessed by demons—the Bible says there were seven of them.

Luke 8:2

2 And certain women, which had been healed of evil spirits and infirmities, Mary called Magdalene, out of whom went seven devils,

> **Flash Card 4.1**

> **TEACHER'S NOTE**
>
> Mary's name *Magdalene* comes from the name of her town, Magdala, which is on the west coast of the Sea of Galilee.

Mary Magdalene was not the only one possessed with demons—Jesus had healed others. Demon possession shows itself differently in different people.

- A man once knelt before Jesus, asking Him to help his demon-possessed son. "Ofttimes he falleth into the fire, and oft into the water," the boy's father told Jesus. How awful that boy's life must have been! Jesus told the demon to come out of the boy, "and the child was cured from that very hour" (Matthew 17:14–17).

- Some people once brought a man to Jesus who couldn't speak because he was demon-possessed. "And when the devil was cast out, the dumb spake…" (Matthew 9:32–33).

- Another man who couldn't speak or see because of demon possession was brought to Jesus. "And he healed him, insomuch that the blind and dumb both spake and saw" (Matthew 12:22).

- Once, as Jesus got off a ship, a demon-possessed man met him. This man, who was possessed by many demons, lived in a graveyard, spent his days and nights crying and cutting himself. People in the village tried to confine him with chains so he couldn't destroy himself, but he broke the chains. Jesus sent the unclean spirits out of the man, and immediately he became a changed man.

- People who were demon-possessed sometimes appeared to be "crazy." (Note: In John 10:20, the Jews accused Jesus of having a demon, because they said He was "mad" (out of his mind).

- There was a demon-possessed man at the synagogue where Jesus was teaching. It seems the man appeared normal until, all of a sudden, he cried out, "Let us alone; what have we to do with thee, thou Jesus of Nazareth?" (Mark 1:24). Jesus commanded the spirit to come out of the man. The spirit cried with a loud voice and came out of the man.

God's Word doesn't tell us what Mary was like when she was demon-possessed, but we know that her life was very difficult. She had seven demons that troubled her all the time. They may have made her appear to be crazy, like some people. She may have had loss of speech or vision, like some. She may have harmed herself, as some did.

Or, Mary may have appeared very normal on the outside, with great pain and torment on the inside. We can be sure that however she acted or whatever she looked like, she desperately needed Jesus to change her life.

2. Mary Magdalene Meets Jesus (Luke 8:2; Mark 16:9)

Jesus taught, preached, and healed people wherever He went; and the people whose lives were changed by Jesus shared their good news with others. The news spread quickly from village to village.

We can only imagine how Mary must have felt when she heard of Jesus' casting out demons. She may have thought, "I wonder if He could help me. It seems nothing will ever help me. I don't feel like I even have power to control my own life—how could someone else do for me what I can't do for myself?"

Or, she may have been very excited and thought, "I have to get to Jesus! I've heard He casts out demons. I'm sure these are demons that are making my life so miserable. I've tried everything. I've tried to live a good life. I've tried to get along with people. I've tried to make it in society, but no matter what I try to do, I totally fail. I need help! And I'm sure Jesus is the one who can help me."

Or, Mary Magdalene may have been so controlled by the seven demons that possessed her that she didn't want anything to do with Jesus. Maybe someone brought her to Jesus, as the man had brought his son (Matthew 17:14–17) or as the people had brought the blind and dumb man (Matthew 12:22).

However she felt, and whatever happened to her to get her to Jesus, at the end of it all, she was so glad she got to Jesus!

Just as Jesus had cast the demons out of other demon-possessed people, He cast the demons out of Mary.

Mark 16:9b

9   ...Mary Magdalene, out of whom he had cast seven devils.

And, when Jesus heals a person, their life is forever changed!

- If they were blind, they now see.

- If they were lame, they now walk.

- If they were deaf, they now hear.

- If they were demon-possessed, they are now free.

- If they were unsaved, they no longer have to pay the penalty for their sin. Jesus makes them new, and clean inside.

3. Mary Magdalene's New Life (Luke 8:3)

The Bible doesn't tell us the exact circumstances of Mary's salvation from sin, but we know it happened. Her life became new in Jesus.

2 Corinthians 5:17

17 Therefore if any man be in Christ, he is a new creature: old things are passed away; behold, all things are become new.

Mary had a new life—a changed life. She was free from the seven demons who had made her so miserable, and she was free from her sin. She didn't look at life the way she used to, now that she knew Jesus.

Flash Card 4.2

Mary was so grateful to Jesus that she chose to give her whole life to Him. She joined the people who followed Jesus on His preaching trips. She wanted Him to continue changing her, and she knew that change would come through being with Him and listening to His Word.

Romans 12:1–2

1 I beseech you therefore, brethren, by the mercies of God, that ye present your bodies a living sacrifice, holy, acceptable unto God, which is your reasonable service.

2 And be not conformed to this world: but be ye transformed by the renewing of your mind, that ye may prove what is that good, and acceptable, and perfect, will of God.

The more time she spent with Jesus, the more she changed.

She used to think about herself, trying to just make it through the day, but she never felt peaceful or happy. Now she thought about Jesus and what He had done for her. How could she show Him her gratefulness?

Galatians 2:20

20 I am crucified with Christ: nevertheless I live; yet not I, but Christ liveth in me: and the life which I now live in the flesh I live by the faith of the Son of God, who loved me, and gave himself for me.

She used to spend her time doing things to try to make herself happy, but all the things she did never really brought her true happiness. Now she gave her time to Jesus. What could she do for Him today?

Ephesians 2:10

10 For we are his workmanship, created in Christ Jesus unto good works, which God hath before ordained that we should walk in them.

She used to spend her money on herself, but buying things she wanted never made her happy for very long. Now she wanted to help provide for Jesus and His disciples. After all, they needed food and clothing, just like everyone else; yet because they spent all their time going from town to town preaching the gospel, they didn't have a regular income. What needs does Jesus have?

Matthew 6:19–21

19 Lay not up for yourselves treasures upon earth, where moth and rust doth corrupt, and where thieves break through and steal:

20 But lay up for yourselves treasures in heaven, where neither moth nor rust doth corrupt, and where thieves do not break through nor steal:

21 For where your treasure is, there will your heart be also.

Mary Magdalene gave from a new heart overflowing with love and gratefulness. Jesus was everything to her.

Colossians 3:1–3

1 If ye then be risen with Christ, seek those things which are above, where Christ sitteth on the right hand of God.

2 Set your affection on things above, not on things on the earth.

3 For ye are dead, and your life is hid with Christ in God.

4. Mary's New Life Continues (Mark 15:40–41)

Mary followed Jesus for the rest of her life. She never stopped serving Him and giving to Him from a heart of gratefulness for her salvation from sin—for her changed life. Mary Magdalene was one of the few people who followed Jesus all the way to the cross.

> **Flash Card 4.3**

Mark 15:40–41

40 There were also women looking on afar off: among whom was Mary Magdalene, and Mary the mother of James the less and of Joses, and Salome;

41 (Who also, when he was in Galilee, followed him, and ministered unto him;) and many other women which came up with him unto Jerusalem.

And Mary still served Jesus after His death on the cross. When Jesus' body had been placed in the tomb, with a huge stone rolled in front of it, Mary still wanted to serve Him. She didn't realize that Jesus was going to rise from the dead, so she went to the tomb after His crucifixion to anoint His body with sweet-smelling spices, as was the custom of her day. But when she got there, the stone had been rolled away.

Mary thought someone had come and taken away Jesus' body, and her heart filled with grief. As she stood outside the tomb weeping, Jesus came and spoke to her.

All the time that Mary Magdalene had followed Jesus, she never dreamed He would reward her so richly! She was the very first person to see Jesus after He had risen from the dead. Her new life was more wonderful and full of blessings than Mary could have ever dreamed.

APPLYING THE STORY

Jesus always changes lives. When someone trusts Him as their Saviour, their life is changed—not necessarily because they try to change, but because that is the nature of God. He changes us from lost to saved, from death to life, from walking in darkness to walking in light.

1 Thessalonians 5:5

5 Ye are all the children of light, and the children of the day: we are not of the night, nor of darkness.

We don't really know if Mary Magdalene lived a life of what we would call "great sin" before she trusted Jesus as her Saviour. We do know that she was possessed of seven demons; and therefore, she had great temptation. That is the nature of the devil—he uses temptation to try to destroy our lives.

1 Peter 5:8

8   Be sober, be vigilant; because your adversary the devil, as a roaring lion, walketh about, seeking whom he may devour:

Mary's life may have been full of huge outward sins that would have made people fear her or think of her as a wicked person. Or, her sins may have been more quiet—sins of the heart. Whatever her life was like, she was a sinner.

Romans 3:23

23   For all have sinned, and come short of the glory of God;

Mary was a sinner, and she needed a new life, because sin brings death. Every sinner (and that is every person who has ever lived) needs a new life—one free from sin and death. That new life is through Jesus Christ.

When Jesus died on the cross, it was to pay the death penalty for our sins. When we believe in His death on the cross and His resurrection to new life, His new life becomes ours. We call that being saved. Salvation assures us of eternal life in Heaven.

Salvation is so much more than just knowing we will have a home in Heaven when we die—although that would be wonderful enough! Salvation allows us to know Jesus Christ—the one Who died for our sins so we wouldn't have to. It makes us new "creatures," or creations. What we used to be isn't what we are anymore.

John 17:3

3   And this is life eternal, that they might know thee the only true God, and Jesus Christ, whom thou hast sent.

This is what changed Mary—knowing Jesus. When she met Jesus, He changed her life, and she was forever changed.

- She wanted to know His Word.

- She wanted to follow Him.

- She wanted to spend time with Him.

- She wanted to give Him thanks.

- She wanted to give her money to help finance His ministry.

- She wanted to obey Him.

- She wanted to serve Him.

- She had a deep love for Him that caused her to follow Him all the way to the cross.

That's the way it is for everyone who trusts Jesus as their Saviour and then follows Him. They want to get to know Him. And the more they know Him, the more their life changes. And the more their life changes, the more they want to serve Him and live for Him, and the more grateful they become.

Salvation is a life transformation. It makes us a new "creation" in Christ. We were under the curse of the penalty of sin, but we are now free from that curse. We no longer serve Satan—we are free to serve Jesus Christ.

The transformation didn't end there for Mary, and it doesn't need to end there for you, either. God wants you to know Him, just as Mary Magdalene knew Jesus; and you can—the same way Mary got to know Him:

- Study His Word.

- Follow Him—ask Him to direct your paths each day.

- Spend time with Him—talk to Him through prayer. Share your joys and sorrows with Him. Ask Him to forgive and cleanse you from the sins you have committed each day (1 John 1:9).

- Remember His goodness to you, and thank Him for it (Psalm 103:2).

- Realize that the money you have comes from Him, and rejoice in giving back to Him.

- Obey His instructions found in the Bible.

- Serve Him by serving others.

- Commit your life to following Him, even when it is difficult.

Jesus transforms the lives of all who trust Him as Saviour. The more you get to know Him, the more obvious and wonderful that transformation will seem to you and to all those around you.

REVIEW GAME/QUESTIONS

Materials Needed

Scissors

White cardstock

Crayola Color Switchers markers

Set Up

Cut out hearts from the white cardstock. With the invisible ink marker, write various point values on each heart. Arrange the hearts on a pocket chart or place in a bag or container.

Playing the Game

Divide the class into two teams. Ask students from Team One a question. If they answer correctly, allow the student to come to the front, choose a heart, and then choose a color from the set of markers. Instruct the student to color the heart to reveal the number of points that will be added to their score. Give a question to Team Two and repeat the process. The team with the most points wins.

Application

It was so fun to see the hearts transform, revealing the points for your teams! It is also wonderful to watch God transform our hearts, like He transformed Mary Magdelene. This week, let Him change your heart when He speaks to you through His Word.

1. What are some "pictures" God gave us to help us understand what He does in us?
   Answer: Answers will vary, but will likely include physical growth, change of seasons, water to ice and steam, life cycle of a butterfly.

2. What is another word for change?
   Answer: Transformation

3. What problem did Mary Magdalene have that she needed Jesus' help for?
   Answer: She was demon-possessed.

4. How many demons did Mary Magdalene have?
   Answer: Seven

5. What were some of the problems that the demon-possessed people had?
   Answer: Loss of vision and speech; some of them harmed themselves; some seemed "crazy."

6. Where did Mary choose to go after she met Jesus?
   Answer: She joined the people who followed Jesus on His preaching trips.

7. Why did Mary go to Jesus' tomb after the crucifixion?
   Answer: To anoint His body with sweet-smelling spices

8. Who did Mary meet outside the tomb?
   Answer: Jesus

9. Why did Mary need a new life?
   Answer: Because she was a sinner, and sin brings death.

10. What are some ways Mary got to know Jesus that are also ways for us to know Him?
    Answer: Answers will vary, but should include: studying the Bible, following Him, spending time with Him, remembering and thanking Him for His goodness, rejoicing in giving money back to God, obeying Him, serving Him, committing your life to following Him.

Teaching the Memory Verse

2 Corinthians 5:17

17 Therefore if any man be in Christ, he is a new creature: old things are passed away; behold, all things are become new.

Materials Needed

Memory Verse Flashcards from Ministry Resource download

Teaching the Verse

Using the Memory Verse Flashcards, repeat the verse several times with the students. Instruct the class to transform their voices each time they recite the verse together.

They can transform their voices by reciting the verse with a Russian, Chinese, British, or Southern accent. They may also transform their voices by plugging their noses or speaking without moving their lips, etc.

OBJECT LESSON
—Beautiful Transformations

Materials Needed

Ice cube trays (trays with patterns,
such as hearts or shapes, would work great)
Pitcher of water

Lesson

Before class, freeze water in the ice cube trays. Place several ice cubes in a container for the class to see. (Be sure to pack the ice cubes in an ice chest during class.)

During the object lesson, show the students the pitcher of water and the frozen ice cubes, pointing out the transformation that takes place with the water once it is frozen.

Variation: You may consider using Jell-O for this illustration. The liquid Jell-O (before refrigeration) can replace the water, and Jell-o that has set in different molds can replace the ice.

Application

When Jesus Christ comes into our lives, we are new creatures. Like the caterpillar that transforms into a butterfly, Jesus transforms our lives into something new and better. Before Christ, our lives were like this water, without direction or purpose. But, once we met Christ, He transformed us like this ice cube. He gave us clear direction and a new purpose. Now, we can live for Him as a new creature in Christ!

CRAFT
—Mary Magdalene Transition Ink Pen

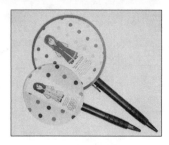

Supplies

Mary Magdalene printable from the
Ministry Resource download
Retractable ink pens (one per student)
Craft glue or double sided tape

Instructions

1. Print the Mary Magdalene printables and cut out the circles.
2. Give each student one of each of the Mary Magdalene circle printables and an ink pen.
3. Instruct the students to attach each circle to the ink pen so that the circles are back to back with the ink pen in the middle.

Application

Instruct the students to rotate Mary before she accepts Christ as Saviour and after she accepts Christ as Saviour. Remind your class that Jesus can bring true and lasting transformation into our lives.

ADDITIONAL RESOURCES

Find the following items on the Ministry Resource download:

*   Coloring Page (for younger children)
*   Activity Page (for older children)
*   Student Take-Home Paper
*   PowerPoint Presentation

Suggested Classroom Schedule

Before Class	Complete attendance record. Provide students with coloring pages/activity pages.
Opening	Welcome
Prayer	Prayer requests and praise reports from the children
Song Time	
Object Lesson	Filled with Power
Song Time	
Memory Verse	Ephesians 6:10
Bible Lesson	Peter
Application/Invitation	Help saved students apply lesson. Invite unsaved students to receive Christ.
Snack	Powerade & Crackers
Review Game/ Questions	
Craft	Peter Puppet
Closing	Give announcements and pray. Distribute take-home papers.

Lesson Five Overview

Peter
Theme—God's Power to Use Us

Scripture
Matthew 4:18–20; 16:21–23

Memory Verse
Ephesians 6:10—*"Finally, my brethren, be strong in the Lord, and in the power of his might."*

Lesson Outline
Introducing the Story
After repeatedly failing and living in his own strength, Peter finally decided he would let the Lord have full control. He learned that without God's Holy Spirit working through him, he was powerless to do anything for the Lord.

Telling the Story
1. **Peter Was Jesus' Disciple** *(Matthew 4:18-20)*
2. **Peter Was Bold While with Jesus** *(Matthew 16:21-23; 26:51-54; Luke 22:31-34; 54-62) —Flashcard 5.1*
3. **Peter Became Discouraged** *(John 21:1-19) —Flashcard 5.2*
4. **Peter Receives the Holy Spirit** *(Acts 1:1-2, 4)*
5. **Peter Walks in the Power of the Holy Spirit** *(Acts 2:5-41) —Flashcard 5.3*

Applying the Story
Through our own power and boldness, we can do things that seem pretty good to us. But through the power of the Holy Spirit, God can do things through us that are greater than anything we can think of!

5 Peter

Theme: God's Power to Use Us

TEACHER'S CHECKLIST

☐ Read Matthew 4:18–20, Matthew 16:21–23, John 21:1–19, Acts 1–2.

☐ Study Lesson Five.

☐ Flash cards 5.1–5.3.

☐ Prepare snack—Powerade & crackers.

☐ Gather for the "Use an Object"—latex gloves.

☐ Gather for object lesson—flashlight and batteries.

☐ Gather for teaching the memory verse—Memory Verse Flashcards and Review Game cards from the Ministry Resource download, timer, small prizes for winners.

☐ Gather for craft—paint sticks, craft sticks, wiggle eyes, 1 yard of two different color fabrics, fine point permanent marker, craft glue, and small rubber band.

☐ Print for review game—*Power Play* cards from the Ministry Resource download.

☐ Print for teaching the memory verse—Memory Verse Flashcards and Review Game cards from the Ministry Resource download.

☐ Print and duplicate Coloring Pages or Activity Pages on the Ministry Resource download (one per student).

☐ Print and duplicate Take-Home Paper on the Ministry Resource download (one per student).

SNACK SUGGESTION

Powerade & Crackers Consider serving individual Powerade bottles with crackers. Alternately, you may want to serve Power Bars to your class. Either option provides the opportunity to remind your class to seek God's power rather than their own.

SCRIPTURES

Matthew 4:18–20

18 And Jesus, walking by the sea of Galilee, saw two brethren, Simon called Peter, and Andrew his brother, casting a net into the sea: for they were fishers.

19 And he saith unto them, Follow me, and I will make you fishers of men.

20 And they straightway left their nets, and followed him.

MEMORY VERSE

Ephesians 6:10 *"Finally, my brethren, be strong in the Lord, and in the power of his might."*

Matthew 16:21–23

21   From that time forth began Jesus to shew unto his disciples, how that he must go unto Jerusalem, and suffer many things of the elders and chief priests and scribes, and be killed, and be raised again the third day.

22   Then Peter took him, and began to rebuke him, saying, Be it far from thee, Lord: this shall not be unto thee.

23   But he turned, and said unto Peter, Get thee behind me, Satan: thou art an offence unto me: for thou savourest not the things that be of God, but those that be of men.

BIBLE LESSON

Introducing the Story

USE AN OBJECT

Bring latex gloves to class and give one or two to each student.

As you describe the abilities gloves have when you place your hand inside, encourage students to put their gloves on.

Then, throughout the story, put on or remove your own gloves at appropriate places.

What is the purpose of a glove? (Allow students to answer.)

Gloves are coverings for our hands. Some gloves we wear in winter to protect our hands from the cold. Some gloves we wear in the garden to protect our hands from dirt and thorns. Some gloves we wear to protect our hands from becoming calloused or injured when working with tools. Some gloves—the kind we have here—protect our hands from germs.

When you place your hand inside a glove, it does everything your hand does. If you point your finger, the glove's finger points. If you clap your hands together, the glove claps. If you pick up a pencil or a piece of paper, the glove picks up the pencil or the paper.

But remove the glove from your hand, and it can't do anything. Your hand can keep doing all kinds of things, but the glove is just an empty glove. With your hand inside it, the glove can do anything your hand can do. Without your hand, the glove is powerless.

Our true story from the Bible is about Peter, one of Jesus' twelve disciples. After repeatedly stumbling, living in his own strength, he finally decided he was going to be like a glove for the Holy Spirit to wear. He learned the hard way that without God's Holy Spirit working through him, he really was powerless to do anything for the Lord.

THE STORY

1. Peter Was Jesus' Disciple (Matthew 4:18–20)

As Jesus walked by the Sea of Galilee, he called to two brothers—Peter and Andrew—who were casting their fishing nets into the sea, "Follow me, and I will make you fishers of men."

Peter and Andrew recognized Him as the Messiah they had been waiting for—the one God promised would save us from our sins—and they immediately left their nets and followed Jesus to become fishers of men instead of fishers of fish.

2. Peter Was Bold While with Jesus (Matthew 16:21–23; 26:51–54; Luke 22:31–34; 54–62)

For the three or so years that Peter followed Jesus before Jesus was crucified, Peter was very brave. He loved Jesus, and he stood up for Him whenever he had a chance.

Once, when Jesus was teaching His disciples about His coming crucifixion and resurrection, the boldness in Peter's heart was so strong that he even argued with Jesus, "No, Lord! This won't happen to you!" Peter didn't want to believe Jesus would be killed.

"You're thinking man's thoughts, not God's thoughts," Jesus answered Peter. "I have to be crucified to pay for the sins of the world" (Matthew 16:21–23).

Later, when the soldiers came to take Jesus to be crucified, boldness to protect Jesus welled up in Peter's heart. Although he knew he was outnumbered by the soldiers, brave Peter decided he would take a stand to protect the Lord. He drew his sword from its sheath, and cut off the ear of Malchus, the high priest's servant.

Flash Card 5.1

"You know, Peter, I could just ask God the Father, and He would send angels to protect me," Jesus said. "If you use your own boldness and strength to fight with swords, you will be killed by the sword. This is God's work and you need to look at things through God's perspective." And Jesus healed Malchus' ear (Matthew 26:51–54; Luke 22:49–51; John 18:10–11).

Earlier, when the disciples were having their last meal with Jesus before He was to be crucified, Jesus told Peter that He knew Satan wanted Peter to fall and not live for Jesus. Peter's boldness rose up in his spirit, and he answered, "Lord, I am ready to go with thee, both into prison, and to death."

Jesus knew Peter was bold when he was with Jesus, and He also knew Peter wasn't going to be so bold when he was alone. "You will deny that you even know me, Peter," Jesus answered. "But I have prayed for you, that your faith will be strengthened and you will one day strengthen the other believers" (Luke 22:31–34).

And, it happened as Jesus had predicted. After Jesus was arrested and was no longer at Peter's side to encourage him, Peter's boldness failed him. When a young girl, much weaker than Peter, said, "This man was with Jesus," Peter was afraid he would be punished for being Jesus' friend, and he said, "I don't even know that man!" The same fear caused Peter to tell two other people that he didn't know Jesus. Peter was so disappointed in himself! (Luke 22:54–62)

3. Peter Became Discouraged (John 21:1–19)

After Jesus was crucified and buried, Peter was discouraged. "I quit," he said. "I have failed the Lord, and I'm going back to fishing. I did it before, and I can do it again. It's just too hard to be a Christian." Peter felt weak and alone. Some of the other disciples followed Peter; and together they went out to sea.

Although Peter gave up on Jesus, Jesus never gave up on Peter.

Hebrews 13:5b

5   …for he hath said, I will never leave thee, nor forsake thee.

Flash Card 5.2

After Jesus' resurrection from the dead, He went to the Sea of Galilee and found Peter and the other disciples fishing, discouraged that they had fished all night and not caught a single fish.

To Peter's great surprise, when he came ashore, he found that Jesus had built a campfire and was grilling fish. "Have breakfast with me," Jesus invited the disciples.

After they ate, Jesus spoke especially to Peter. "My purpose for your life hasn't changed at all. You are still to be a fisher and leader of men.

Peter must have said to himself, "Wow! Jesus still loves me! He really did rise from the dead. The power over death is also the power over sin, and it is the power to help me do and become what God wants me to be."

Romans 8:11

11   But if the Spirit of him that raised up Jesus from the dead dwell in you, he that raised up Christ from the dead shall also quicken your mortal bodies by his Spirit that dwelleth in you.

Imagine what Peter must have told the other disciples: "Okay guys, I'm done with fishing. I know I told you I was going back to fishing, but Jesus has found me and forgiven me. I'm not exactly sure what His whole purpose is for my life, but He told me He has a plan for my life, and it's a lot greater than fishing. He called me to be a fisher of men three years ago, and a fisher of men is what I'm going to be."

4. Peter Receives the Holy Spirit (Acts 1:1–2, 4)

And that's what Peter did. He returned to Jerusalem and joined the other ten disciples. (Judas had betrayed Jesus and had hung himself.) Jesus met with the disciples and others several times over the forty days between His resurrection and His returning to Heaven.

The last time Jesus met with them, He said, "You will receive power from the Holy Ghost and will be witnesses for me in Jerusalem, Judaea, Samaria, and to the farthest corners of the earth." And then Jesus was taken up to Heaven.

The eleven disciples joined many other disciples (followers) of Jesus, about one hundred twenty in all. Together they waited for the Holy Spirit to come upon them as Jesus had promised, so they would have His power to be witnesses for Jesus.

One day, as they were together, the Holy Spirit came on the disciples with power so great that He enabled them to speak in other languages so they could share the gospel with others who didn't speak the Hebrew language they spoke.

5. Peter Walks in the Power of the Holy Spirit (Acts 2:5–41)

Peter had a new boldness—not the boldness of a strong man who did his own will, but the boldness that the Holy Spirit of God gives a person to do God's will.

Less than two short months after Jesus had so lovingly talked to Peter on the seashore, God gave Peter the boldness, courage, desire, and passion to preach.

Flash Card 5.3

When people heard about the disciples being able to speak in languages they had never learned, but that the Holy Spirit had enabled them to speak, thousands came to see this for themselves. The Bible says people from many different languages heard the disciples speak in their language.

Some of the people said, "These men must be drunk!"

Peter, filled with the power of the Holy Spirit, boldly proclaimed, "No, these men aren't drunk. This is what the prophet Joel meant in the Old Testament when he said God said He would show great wonders."

And then Peter went on to preach his first sermon. He told the listeners that they had crucified Jesus, and he preached the gospel. As Peter preached through the power of the Holy Spirit, thousands who listened were convicted of their sin, and three thousand people trusted Jesus as their Saviour that very day; and a church was begun in Jerusalem.

"Having the Holy Spirit with me is just like Jesus Himself being with me," Peter realized. "I can do anything He leads me to do when He's with me!"

John 14:26

26 But the Comforter, which is the Holy Ghost, whom the Father will send in my name, he shall teach you all things, and bring all things to your remembrance, whatsoever I have said unto you.

1 John 5:7

7 For there are three that bear record in heaven, the Father, the Word, and the Holy Ghost: and these three are one.

The Holy Spirit enabled Peter to do many other things:

- He became a leader of the church in Jerusalem (Galatians 2:9, Cephas = Peter).

- He became the counselor of other pastors (Acts 15:1–11).

- He stayed through persecution to strengthen other believers and wrote two books of the Bible to strengthen persecuted churches (1 and 2 Peter).

- He was given the power to heal people who had diseases (Acts 5:15–16).

No longer did Peter stumble through life trusting in his own wisdom and strength. He now lived through the power of the Holy Spirit of God, and he saw God do mighty works through him.

APPLYING THE STORY

Peter was a leader of the disciples. He was the one who took charge, often spoke up first, and one sent on special errands by Jesus. He was one of the disciples with whom Jesus spent the most time. Peter saw Jesus perform miracles, and Peter boldly stood up for the Lord.

Peter probably looked pretty strong to others, as he lived in his own strength, trusting in his own boldness. People likely thought "Oh wow, Peter must have the power of God on him. The Lord sure does a lot through Peter!"

But being in charge, being the most popular, or being the loudest or strongest doesn't accomplish God's will. God's will can only be accomplished through the power of God. Things that are accomplished through the power of God bring glory to God, rather than to people or other things.

Isaiah 42:8

8   I am the LORD: that is my name: and my glory will I not give to another, neither my praise to graven images.

When Peter's boldness didn't come through God, it came through what he stirred up in himself. One of the problems with trusting in our own boldness and strength as Peter did is that it is no match for Satan, whose purpose is to destroy us.

1 Peter 5:8

8   Be sober, be vigilant; because your adversary the devil, as a roaring lion, walketh about, seeking whom he may devour:

When Peter cut off Malchus' ear, Jesus told him that God's work needed to be done through God. If we try to overcome Satan in our own boldness and strength, we will fail. We, like Peter in this case, will not understand God's will; and we may be doing something to prevent what God wants to do through a situation.

Another problem with trusting in our own boldness and strength is that we don't get to see the wonderful work God wants to do through us.

1 Corinthians 2:5

5   That your faith should not stand in the wisdom of men, but in the power of God.

Through our own power and boldness, we can do things that seem pretty good to us. But through the power of the Holy Spirit, God can do things through us that are greater than anything we can think of!

We receive the Holy Spirit the moment we trust Jesus as our Saviour from sin. He immediately comes to live in us.

Romans 8:9b

9   Now if any man have not the Spirit of Christ, he is none of his.

Romans 8:16

16   The Spirit itself beareth witness with our spirit, that we are the children of God:

Ephesians 1:13–14

13   In whom ye also trusted, after that ye heard the word of truth, the gospel of your salvation: in whom also after that ye believed, ye were sealed with that holy Spirit of promise,

14   Which is the earnest of our inheritance until the redemption of the purchased possession, unto the praise of his glory.

It's amazing to realize that the Holy Spirit of God actually lives in all those who are saved! But although each saved person has the Holy Spirit living in him or her, we can still choose to live by our own power, thinking our own thoughts, and choosing our own way. That's how Peter often lived at the beginning. Then, after he received the Holy Spirit, Peter chose to live by the Holy Spirit's power. We have the same choice Peter had:

- When we choose to walk the path that seems comfortable to us, rather than following God's commands, we are not walking in the power of the Holy Spirit (Galatians 5:16, 25).

- When we choose to live in ways that are against God's instructions in the Bible (anger, immorality, dishonesty, stealing, ungodly lifestyle and speech, etc.) we grieve the Holy Spirit (Ephesians 4:1–32).

- When we choose to ignore the Holy Spirit's leading in our lives we quench (extinguish; put out) the Holy Spirit (1 Thessalonians 5:19).

- When we choose to trust the wisdom of man, we are not trusting in the power of the Holy Spirit (1 Corinthians 2:5).

Galatians 5:22–23 gives us a kind of gauge to help us determine whether or not we are walking in the Holy Spirit.

Galatians 5:22–23

22   But the fruit of the Spirit is love, joy, peace, longsuffering, gentleness, goodness, faith,

23   Meekness, temperance: against such there is no law.

These are the "fruit of the Spirit" that God produces in our lives when we walk in the Spirit.

TEACHER'S NOTE

The indwelling of the Holy Spirit at salvation assures us of eternal security.

Romans 8:9 teaches that if a person doesn't have the Holy Spirit, he doesn't belong to God. Since all believers belong to God, all believers *must* have the Holy Spirit.

Romans 8:16 teaches that the Holy Spirit witnesses with our spirit that we are God's children.

Ephesians 1:13–14 teach that we are sealed (*Sealed* means *confirmation*) by the Holy Spirit—that He is the earnest (as in real estate) of our inheritance, assuring us that God will fulfill His promise of eternal life to all who trust in Him.

You may also wish to study:

John 7:37–39
1 Corinthians 3:16; 6:19
2 Corinthians 1:21, 22; 5:5
Ephesians 4:30

Maybe you haven't been living in the power of the Holy Spirit and have failed the Lord, like Peter. The good thing is that if you, like Peter, feel you have disappointed the Lord and have given up on Him, He has never given up on you. He is there, just waiting to walk with you and to give you power to live your life through His Holy Spirit. His power will enable you to do so many things that you can't truly do in your own strength:

- Witness for Him (Matthew 28:19–20).
- Go to Him for comfort (John 14:16).
- Overcome temptation and sin (Romans 8:2).
- Understand the Bible (1 Corinthians 2:13).
- Become more like Jesus (2 Corinthians 3:18).
- Walk in freedom (2 Corinthians 3:17).
- Be strong in your spirit (Ephesians 3:16).
- Have joy (1 Thessalonians 1:6).
- Obey the truth (1 Peter 1:22).

TEACHER'S NOTE

You may wish to choose one or more from the list of things the Holy Spirit does in and through us. You will find many more as you study the Holy Spirit in the Bible.

Be sure to remind your students that the Holy Spirit only lives in those who are saved—salvation is the first step to a relationship with God.

REVIEW GAME/QUESTIONS

Materials Needed
Power Play cards from the Ministry Resource download

Set up
Print and cut the *Power Play* cards and arrange on a pocket chart or in bag or container.

Playing the Game
Divide the class into two teams. When a team answers a question correctly, allow a student to pick a Power Play card. The team must follow the instructions given on the card. Continue playing, alternating between teams.

The team with the most points at the end of the game wins.

1. Where does a glove get its power?
   Answer: From the hand inside it

2. Who did Peter and Andrew recognize Jesus as?
   Answer: Their Messiah

3. What were some times when Peter was bold when he was with Jesus?
    Answer: When Jesus was teaching about His crucifixion; when Jesus told Peter that Satan wanted him to die, and not live for Jesus; when the soldiers captured Jesus and Peter cut off Malchus' ear.

4. Why did Peter go back to fishing?
    Answer: Because he was so ashamed that he had told people he didn't know Jesus; Peter didn't think Jesus could use him any longer

5. After Jesus' resurrection, where did He find Peter?
    Answer: Fishing on the Sea of Galilee

6. Where did Peter's boldness come from before he had the Holy Spirit?
    Answer: His boldness came from what he stirred up in himself.

7. Where did Peter's new boldness come from?
    Answer: The power of the Holy Spirit

8. What were some of the things that the Holy Spirit enabled Peter to do?
    Answer: Answers will vary, but should include: Peter became the leader of the church in Jerusalem, became a counselor of other pastors, stayed through persecution to strengthen other believers, wrote two books of the Bible to strengthen persecuted churches, was given power to heal people

9. Name some of the fruits of the Spirit.
    Answer: Love, joy, peace, longsuffering, gentleness, goodness, faith, meekness, temperance

10. What are some things the Holy Spirit's power will enable you to do?
    Answer: Answers will vary, but should include: witnessing for Him, going to Him for comfort, overcoming temptation and sin, understanding the Bible, becoming more like Jesus, walking in freedom, being strong in your spirit, having joy, and obeying the truth.

Teaching the Memory Verse

Ephesians 6:10

10   Finally, my brethren, be strong in the Lord, and in the power of his might.

Materials Needed

Memory Verse Flashcards from the Ministry Resource download

Two sets of the Review Game cards

Timer

Small prizes for winners

Teaching the Verse

Print the Memory Verse Flashcards and two sets of the Review Game cards (containing one word on each card).

Review the verse together several times as a class, using the Memory Verse Flashcards.

When students are familiar with the verse, divide the class into teams, and invite one student from each team to come to the front. The students from each team will be given a stack of Review Game cards (scrambled, so the words are not in order). Use the timer to see who can arrange the Review Game cards on a pocket chart in correct order in the least amount of time. (A treat can be rewarded to each student who wins the individual races.)

Continue with several rounds, allowing as many students to participate as possible. The team who wins the most rounds wins.

Variation: A class assistant can help tally the total amount of time for each team, and the team who used the least amount of time throughout the entire game wins.

OBJECT LESSON—Filled with Power

Materials Needed

Flashlight

Batteries

Lesson

The flashlight represents our lives. We have great potential to be used of God to point others to Him. But, we need to be filled with a power source (represented by the batteries) in order to be used of Him effectively.

Application

Living without Jesus is like trying to use a flashlight without batteries. We can't live for Christ or serve Him in our own strength and power. We need him to fill us with His Holy Spirit and enable us to accomplish His will.

ADDITIONAL RESOURCES

Find the following items on the Ministry Resource download:

- Coloring Page (for younger children)
- Activity Page (for older children)
- Student Take-Home Paper
- PowerPoint Presentation

CRAFT—Peter Puppet

Supplies

Paint sticks
Craft sticks
Wiggle eyes
1 yard of two different color fabrics (yields 30 puppets)
Fine point permanent marker
Craft glue (or low temp glue gun & glue sticks)
Small rubber band

Instructions

1. For the coat—cut a 12 inch square from the material (Cut a 1/2 inch incision in the middle).
2. For the belt—cut a 4 inch by 1/2 inch strip from the material.
3. For the hat—cut a 3 inch square from the material.
4. Give each student, 1 paint stick, 1 craft stick, 2 wiggle eyes, 1 coat, 1 belt, and 1 hat.
5. Glue the craft stick to the paint stick horizontally to make the arms.
6. Have the students put the coat on the paint stick (inserting into the hole in the middle).
7. Tie the belt just under the arms (craft stick) of the puppet.
8. Glue the hat on the top of the paint stick & put a rubber band to secure the hat.
9. Glue the wiggle eyes on.
10. Using a permanent marker, draw a nose and mouth.

Application

Just as our hands fill this puppet and enable it to do what we desire, we should let the Holy Spirit fill and empower us to do what He desires in our lives.

Suggested Classroom Schedule

Before Class	Complete attendance record. Provide students with coloring pages/activity pages.
Opening	Welcome
Prayer	Prayer requests and praise reports from the children
Song Time	
Memory Verse	Colossians 1:10
Song Time	
Object Lesson	See the Need
Bible Lesson	Tabitha
Application/Invitation	Help saved students apply lesson. Invite unsaved students to receive Christ.
Snack	Button Cookies with Licorice Thread
Review Game/ Questions	
Craft	Acts of Kindness
Closing	Give announcements and pray. Distribute take-home papers.

Lesson Six Overview

Tabitha
Theme—Choosing God

Scripture
Acts 9:36–42

Memory Verse
Colossians 1:10—*"That ye might walk worthy of the Lord unto all pleasing, being fruitful in every good work, and increasing in the knowledge of God;"*

Lesson Outline
Introducing the Story

Today's true lesson is about a special woman who was a lot like us—she noticed others' needs. But, she was also a lot like Jesus—she did what she could to meet those needs. She was a servant.

Telling the Story

1. **Tabitha Did Good Deeds** *(Acts 9:36)*
   —*Flashcard 6.1*

2. **Tabitha's Death** *(Acts 9:37)*

3. **Peter Mourns Widows at Joppa** *(Acts 9:38–39)*
   —*Flashcard 6.2*

4. **Peter Raises Tabitha from the Dead** *(Acts 9:40–41)*
   —*Flashcard 6.3*

5. **People Are Saved** *(Acts 9:42)*

Applying the Story

We all see people with needs, just like Tabitha did. Let's be like Tabitha who prayed for the needs, and then she did what she could to meet those needs.

LESSON SIX
Tabitha
Theme: Choosing God

TEACHER'S CHECKLIST

- ☐ Read Acts 9:36–42.
- ☐ Study Lesson Six.
- ☐ Flash cards 6.1—6.3.
- ☐ Prepare snack—Button Cookies with Licorice Thread.
- ☐ Gather for "Use an Object"—cloth bag with pieces of material.
- ☐ Gather for object lesson— paper and props for assistants acting as "people in need."
- ☐ Gather for review game—two bags of clothes.
- ☐ Gather for teaching the memory verse—Memory Verse Flashcards and memory verse shirt templates from the Ministry Resource download, twine, and clothespins.
- ☐ Gather for craft—scraps of material, Acts of Kindness cards from the Ministry Resource download, Chinese take out food boxes, scissors, craft glue.
- ☐ Print for teaching the memory verse—Memory Verse Flashcards and memory verse shirt templates from the Ministry Resource download.
- ☐ Print and duplicate Coloring Pages or Activity Pages on the Ministry Resource download (one per student).
- ☐ Print and duplicate Take-Home Paper on the Ministry Resource download (one per student).

SCRIPTURES

Acts 9:36–42

36 Now there was at Joppa a certain disciple named Tabitha, which by interpretation is called Dorcas: this woman was full of good works and almsdeeds which she did.

37 And it came to pass in those days, that she was sick, and died: whom when they had washed, they laid her in an upper chamber.

MEMORY VERSE

Colossians 1:10
"That ye might walk worthy of the Lord unto all pleasing, being fruitful in every good work, and increasing in the knowledge of God;"

38 And forasmuch as Lydda was nigh to Joppa, and the disciples had heard that Peter was there, they sent unto him two men, desiring him that he would not delay to come to them.

39 Then Peter arose and went with them. When he was come, they brought him into the upper chamber: and all the widows stood by him weeping, and shewing the coats and garments which Dorcas made, while she was with them.

40 But Peter put them all forth, and kneeled down, and prayed; and turning him to the body said, Tabitha, arise. And she opened her eyes: and when she saw Peter, she sat up.

41 And he gave her his hand, and lifted her up, and when he had called the saints and widows, presented her alive.

42 And it was known throughout all Joppa; and many believed in the Lord.

BIBLE LESSON

Introducing the Story

TEACHER'S TIP

As class members suggest examples, jot them down. They will come in handy during the application part of this lesson.

As we go about our days, we sometimes notice needs that other people have. What are some needs you notice in others' lives? (Allow students to give examples.)

We may notice someone on the playground who doesn't have a warm jacket when the weather gets cold. Or we may notice a student in the cafeteria who doesn't have a lunch, or whose lunch has hardly anything in it to eat. Or we may notice someone at church who doesn't have a Bible. Or we may notice someone carrying things that look much too heavy or bulky for one person to carry by themselves. We may notice that our mother has had a hard day and could use help with the supper dishes. (Also affirm the suggestions students have already mentioned.)

God is pleased when we focus our eyes and our thoughts on the needs of others, rather than thinking only of ourselves. He tells us in His Word that Jesus did exactly that—He lived to serve others, rather than Himself. And God instructs us to do the same.

TEACHER'S TIP

You may wish to ask students to cite some needs Jesus met in the gospels. These would include:

- healing a blind man
- healing lepers
- turning water into wine
- sharing spiritual truths etc.

Philippians 2:4–5

4 Look not every man on his own things, but every man also on the things of others.

5 Let this mind be in you, which was also in Christ Jesus:

When Jesus noticed needs other people had, He not only thought about those needs, but He did whatever it took to actually meet those needs. He served others.

It's easy for us to feel sorry for a person, and even to think of kind ways to meet their needs. But it's also easy for us to get busy with something else and then just forget about the kind plans we had to help that person.

We don't plan to forget about them. We just get so busy with other activities.

Today's true story from the Bible is about a special woman who was a lot like us—she noticed others' needs. She was also a lot like Jesus—she did what she could to meet those needs. She was a servant.

This woman was called by two names. Her Greek name was Dorcas, and her Hebrew name was Tabitha.

The Story

1. Tabitha Did Good Deeds (Acts 9:36)

Now, it doesn't just happen out of nowhere that a person becomes a servant. It is a choice a person makes. Imagine Tabitha sitting in church one day and silently thanking God for His kindness to her. "Thank You, Father, for giving Your Son to die on the cross to pay for my sins. Thank You for giving me this wonderful church—for our pastor who teaches us Your Word, and for friends who love You, and who also love me. Thank you for taking care of all my needs, Lord. You are so good to me!"

At the end of the service, Tabitha talked with people she knew, and she also introduced herself to visitors who had come to church.

"I'm Tabitha," she said to a visitor, "and I'm so glad to meet you." The visitor introduced herself, and as they talked, Tabitha discovered that the woman was a widow. Her husband had died a year earlier, and she was having trouble making enough money to provide food and clothing for her three children and herself.

"I'm so sorry," Tabitha's eyes filled with tears as she thought about the needs of this poor family. "May God bless you."

As Tabitha walked home, she thought about the woman she had met. "It's no wonder her dress was ragged. Her poor family doesn't have enough money to meet all their needs. Her children's clothes were mostly too small for them. They don't have enough money to get new clothes when they grow out of the ones they are wearing. Oh, it's too bad they don't have a husband and father to take care of them!"

All the rest of the day, Tabitha thought about the poor widow and her children. Tears came to her eyes again, and she had a big lump in her throat as

TEACHER'S NOTE

Tabitha is a Hebrew name, meaning *gazelle* (or, something we would be more familiar with would be *deer*.) Our text also gives us the Greek translation of her name—*Dorcas.*

Name meanings in Scripture are often significant. In Tabitha's case, it is obvious that she was (as we would think of a deer) a gentle, pleasant person.

ACT IT OUT

Consider calling on students to demonstrate the following possible scenarios with Tabitha and those she served.

she thought about their needs. Her heart was heavy as she realized they didn't have pretty, comfortable clothes to keep them warm.

As she lay in bed that night, Tabitha prayed for the widow's family. "Dear Lord, please remind this family of Your love for them. Please provide clothing for them that is warm—without holes or rips."

When Tabitha awoke in the morning, her first thoughts were of the widow. "I'm not going to just keep on feeling sorry for this family," Tabitha said to herself. "I'm going to do something about it—and I'm going to do it before I forget and get busy doing something else."

She reached into a big cloth bag and pulled out a few large pieces of brightly colored fabric she had woven. "This will be plenty to sew an outfit for each member of the family."

As Tabitha cut the fabric, she sang songs of thanksgiving to the Lord. As she sewed the cut out fabric together into pieces of clothing, she prayed for each member of the widow's family. Her heart was filled with joy as she thought about the happiness her gifts would bring to the widow and her children.

The widow couldn't believe her eyes the next Sunday, as Tabitha opened her cloth bag and pulled out the beautiful outfits she had made. "I don't know how to thank you for these wonderful, beautiful gifts," the widow cried, as she hugged her new dress to herself. "It has cost you a great deal of time and money to make these garments for us. You're such a servant. I wish I could do something to repay you."

"Oh, no—I don't want anything in return," Tabitha answered. "My mother taught me how to sew, and God has provided for me. It brings me joy to share what God and others have given me."

"Wow! I'm glad I didn't just feel sorry for the widow's family," Tabitha thought as she journeyed back to her home. "I'm glad I did something about their needs."

Tabitha kept on noticing the needs of others. "Oh, there's a widow who doesn't have a coat!" And she went home and made her the most beautiful coat the widow had ever seen.

"That boy doesn't have a father, and his shirt is much too small. I'm sure his mother doesn't have enough money to provide a new shirt for him." And she went home and made him a new, bright shirt that he was proud to wear.

"My friend hasn't had a new dress in years," Tabitha said out loud to herself, as she thought about another widow. "I'm going to make her four beautiful dresses, and she can wear a different one each Sunday of the month.

The weeks, months, and years went by; and Tabitha continued watching for the needs of others—especially the widows and their families. And she kept serving them and meeting their needs.

USE AN OBJECT

Bring a cloth bag full of material that you can use to demonstrate as you teach this portion of the lesson.

Flash Card 6.1

Everyone loved Tabitha, and her life was happy and full, because she was full of good works!

Acts 9:36b

36 ...this woman was full of good works and almsdeeds which she did.

Colossians 1:10

10 That ye might walk worthy of the Lord unto all pleasing, being fruitful in every good work, and increasing in the knowledge of God;

TEACHER'S NOTE

almsdeeds —acts of charity; charitable gifts.

Time passed, and Tabitha kept serving. Every day she noticed someone's need, and she made something or did something helpful for them. Sometimes she brought them food, and always she shared God's love with them. She was so happy!

Acts 20:35

35 I have shewed you all things, how that so labouring ye ought to support the weak, and to remember the words of the Lord Jesus, how he said, It is more blessed to give than to receive.

2. Tabitha's Death (Acts 9:37)

But one day, Tabitha became very sick, and she soon died. Her body was prepared for her burial, and she was laid in an upstairs room before the funeral.

"Somehow, I feel like we should go to Peter (Do you remember Peter? We learned about him last week. He was a preacher who had been one of Jesus' twelve disciples.) and ask him to come," one of the disciples (followers of Jesus Christ) suggested. Everyone agreed, and two men went to the nearby town of Lydda, where Peter had been preaching, to ask him to come to Joppa, where Tabitha's body lay.

3. Peter Mourns with Widows at Joppa (Acts 9:38–39)

When Peter climbed the stairs to the upstairs room, he was met by all the widows of the church. The widows had lost a dear friend. She had not only made them coats and garments, but she had listened to the burdens of their hearts and shared words of comfort and love with them.

Flash Card 6.2

James 1:27

27 Pure religion and undefiled before God and the Father is this, To visit the fatherless and widows in their affliction, and to keep himself unspotted from the world.

One by one the widows came to Peter. They wanted to tell him how loving and giving Tabitha had been, and how much they missed her; but they were weeping because of their grief, and the words just wouldn't come out. So, they just showed Peter the beautiful clothing Tabitha had made for them.

Peter looked at the grieving widows, and he looked at the clothing they wore and the coats they held out to him in their arms; and he understood the whole story of Tabitha's life, without a word being spoken to him.

"This was a woman who served others," Peter thought. "She didn't just feel sorry for others in need—she met their needs.

"This room is full of poor widows who don't have enough money to provide for their families, but here they stand in beautiful clothes such as would be worn by women with husbands who have good jobs. And I can see by their sorrow that Tabitha not only made them clothes, but she encouraged their hearts. Tabitha had devoted her life to serving others."

Proverbs 31:31

31 Give her of the fruit of her hands; and let her own works praise her in the gates.

5. Peter Raises Tabitha from the Dead (Acts 9:40–41)

"I need to talk to the Lord," Peter said to himself, and he motioned for all the people in the room to go back downstairs.

When he was alone in the room, Peter knelt down and prayed to God. "Lord, what is your plan? Is Tabitha's work on this earth finished?"

Peter heard the Lord in his heart, and he knew what to do. He turned toward Tabitha's body and said, "Tabitha, arise."

Tabitha immediately opened her eyes, and when she saw Peter, she sat up. Peter reached his hand out to her. "Welcome back to life, Tabitha!" She took Peter's hand, and she stood up.

Peter called the widows and church family to come back upstairs, and they couldn't believe their eyes. Tabitha was alive!

Flash Card 6.3

6. People Are Saved (Acts 9:42)

"Can you believe it? Tabitha died, but God sent Peter to bring her back to life," all the widows told their family and friends. "And now she's back, doing what she always did—helping the poor and needy. God is so good!"

"Now I believe in God," many of the people answered. "I believe in the God Tabitha trusted and served. I believe His Word!"

APPLYING THE STORY

We all see people with needs, just like Tabitha did. And we all feel sorry for those needs. We often think of ways we could help the people with the needs. But sadly, we often forget.

Sometimes the needs we see are physical needs, like a need for a new coat, shoes, or even a meal. They may need someone to lend them a hand with a chore they have to do—raking leaves, shoveling snow, washing dishes.

Sometimes the needs we see are needs of the heart. Someone may be friendless, and we think of asking them to play a game with us. They may be lonely, in a nursing home, and we think of visiting them or writing them a note. They may be going through something hard in their family, and we think of just letting them share their heart.

Sometimes the needs we see are spiritual needs. They may not know Jesus as their Saviour, and we think of giving them a tract or sharing the gospel with them. They may be struggling with some sin, and we think of encouraging them and helping them with God's Word.

What did Tabitha do when she saw needs? (Allow students to answer.) She prayed for the needs, and then she did what she could to meet those needs—and she did it before she forgot!

That's what we need to do, as well.

- "Dear Lord, it's getting cold out, and Chelsea's coat is too small for her. Please provide a warm coat for her."

  "Mom, may I give Chelsea my extra coat? She doesn't have one that fits, and I think mine would be just right for her."

- "Lord, Mom looks so tired. She has worked so hard all day, and she made this good meal for us. Please help her to be able to rest."

  "Mom, you go take a nice warm bath and read a book for a while. I'll do these dishes."

TEACHER'S TIP

Use illustrations and remedies to which your class would relate.

This is when you would use the examples class members gave at the beginning of the lesson:

"What could you do when you notice a particular need they suggested?"

- "Oh, Lord, I feel so sorry for poor Mrs. Johnson in the nursing home. Her family lives far away, and hardly anyone goes to visit her. Please encourage her heart."

  "Mom, will you take me to visit Mrs. Johnson tomorrow after school?"

- "Lord, Adyn always seems so alone. No one asks him to play with them at recess, and no one ever picks him to be on their team. Please help him to have friends."

  "Hey, Adyn, do you want to play four-square with us at recess?"

- "Lord, Steven just keeps struggling with that same sin over and over, and it's causing all kinds of problems in his life. Please help him to get victory over it."

  "Thanks for sharing your problem with me, Steven—that's really tough to go through. I went through something like that last year, and it was related to this certain sin I struggled with. Let me show you some things from the Bible that God used in my life."

- "Lord, I don't believe Jessica knows you as her Saviour. Please work in her heart and draw her to You."

  "Jessica, I want to share with you the most wonderful thing that ever happened to me—the most wonderful thing in the whole world…"

God didn't tell us in the Bible what Tabitha looked like—maybe she was beautiful, and maybe she wasn't. He didn't tell us what kind of house she lived in—maybe it was fancy, and maybe it wasn't. He didn't tell us her age—maybe she was old, and maybe she was quite young.

Proverbs 31:30

30　Favour is deceitful, and beauty is vain: but a woman that feareth the LORD, she shall be praised.

God did tell us that Tabitha did something every one of us can do. It doesn't matter if we are rich or poor, beautiful or plain. We can all do good works.

2 Corinthians 8:11–12

11　Now therefore perform the doing of it; that as there was a readiness to will, so there may be a performance also out of that which ye have.

12　For if there be first a willing mind, it is accepted according to that a man hath, and not according to that he hath not.

REVIEW GAME/QUESTIONS

Materials Needed

Two bags of oversized or adult sized shirts, sweaters, and coats. (All types can be incorporated, such as pullovers or button ups, as these will add various levels of difficulty to the relay race.)

Set up

Divide your class into two teams and arrange in lines (one line for each team) to participate in a relay. Place one bag of clothes for each team at the front of the room, several yards directly in front of the students' lines.

Playing the Game

Ask a review question to the first students in line on each team. Once the question has been given, the students can race to the bags of clothing, reach in and select a garment, put it completely on (fastening snaps, securing buttons, etc.), run back to their respective lines, and then answer the question.

The first student to answer the question correctly and completely be clothed in the new article of clothing receives a point for their team. The team with the most points at the end of the game wins.

1. In what way was Tabitha like Jesus?
   Answer: She did what she could to meet others' needs.

2. What was Tabitha's name in Greek?
   Answer: Dorcas

3. What did Tabitha do to make sure she didn't forget to meet a need she had noticed?
   Answer: She did something to help right away.

4. What does the word almsdeeds mean?
   Answer: Acts of charity

5. Where was Tabitha's body laid after she died?
   Answer: In an upstairs room

6. What was the name of the preacher the disciples asked to come to Joppa after Tabitha died?
   Answer: Peter

7. Who met Peter in the upper room?
   Answer: The widows of the church

8. How did Peter know Tabitha had lived the life of a servant?
    Answer: The widows grieved so much because of her death, and they showed him the garments she had made.

9. What was something Tabitha did that every one of us can do, no matter how much money we have or what we look like?
    Answer: Good works

10. What good work are you going to do today?
    Answer: Answers will vary.

Teaching the Memory Verse

Colossians 1:10

10 That ye might walk worthy of the Lord unto all pleasing, being fruitful in every good work, and increasing in the knowledge of God;

Materials Needed

Memory Verse Flashcards from the Ministry Resource download
Memory verse shirt templates
Twine
Clothespins

Set Up

Print the Memory Verse Flashcards and the shirt template containing the words of the verse. Cut out the shirts.
Affix twine or small rope across the board and using clothes pins, arrange the shirts on the twine.

Teaching the Verse

Instruct the students to read the verse together as a class several times. Once they have become familiar with the verse, allow students to remove one shirt each time they repeat the verse. Continue reciting the verse until no t-shirts remain on the clothesline.

OBJECT LESSON—See the Need

Materials Needed

Several pieces of paper rolled into a funnel shape with a dime-sized hole at the end. These will serve as special scopes used to navigate an obstacle course.

Props for those who represent "people in need".

Lesson

Before class, arrange for your helpers to participate in this object lesson. They will represent people who are in need. You can create scenarios best suited to your class, but some examples could include the following:

- One assistant can be a mom struggling with an unruly baby.

- Another assistant can represent a boy who has just dropped his backpack, spilling all the contents on to the floor.

- Another assistant can be dressed as an elderly grandparent who is struggling to cross a street.

- Your final assistant can be a lonely child who has no friends at recess.

Your assistants (or students in your class, if you don't have enough helpers) will be strategically arranged at the front of the classroom to form an obstacle course.

Ask for two or three student volunteers to participate in this object lesson. They will step out of the room with a helper as the obstacle course is set up and will each be given two funnel shaped "glasses" that they will hold up to their eyes.

As they re-enter the classroom, instruct the students to walk through the obstacle course, using only their tunnel vision. Give them a focal point to walk toward, located at the end of the course.

Application

After the students have reached their focal point, allow them to remove their tunnel vision "glasses" and see what they passed as they walked through the course. Show them each person who needed help along their way, who they could not see because they were so focused on getting to their destination.

If time allows, invite the class to share ways they could serve and help those who were needy on the obstacle course.

Encourage the students to remove their own tunnel vision and to go through the upcoming week with eyes open and alert to help those in need.

CRAFT—Acts of Kindness

Supplies

Scraps of material (Cut into 2 inch squares—1/2 yard provides enough material for 30 students.)
Acts of Kindness cards from Ministry Resource download
Small Chinese take out food boxes
Scissors
Craft glue

Instructions

1. Print out the Bible verses for each student and cut into small cards.
2. Give each student a pair of scissors, a 2-inch square of material, acts of kindness cards, and a Chinese take out box.
3. Instruct the students to glue the material to the outside of the box.
4. Insert the acts of kindness cards into the box.

Application

Encourage the students to pull out a different act of kindness each day this week and do them: serving the Lord by serving others.

ADDITIONAL RESOURCES

Find the following items on the Ministry Resource download:

- Coloring Page (for younger children)
- Activity Page (for older children)
- Student Take-Home Paper
- PowerPoint Presentation

Suggested Classroom Schedule

Before Class		Complete attendance record. Provide students with coloring pages/activity pages.
Opening		Welcome
Prayer		Prayer requests and praise reports from the children
Song Time		
Memory Verse		Luke 16:10a
Song Time		
Object Lesson		Faithful Friend
Bible Lesson		Stephen
Application/Invitation		Help saved students apply lesson. Invite unsaved students to receive Christ.
Snack		Heavenly Clouds
Review Game/ Questions		
Craft		Faithfulness Containers
Closing		Give announcements and pray. Distribute take-home papers.

Lesson Seven Overview

Stephen
Theme—Faithfulness

Scripture
Acts 6:1-7

Memory Verse
Luke 16:10a—*"He that is faithful in that which is least is faithful also in much."*

Lesson Outline
Introducing the Story
Along with all the wonderful blessings of the Christian life, we will also experience what Jesus called the blessing of persecution. The man in today's true story from the Bible suffered great persecution, and through it he was faithful to Jesus.

Telling the Story
1. **Stephen Chosen as a Deacon** *(Acts 6:1-5)*
    —Flashcard 7.1

2. **Stephen Used of God** *(Acts 6:8)*

3. **Stephen Brought into Questioning** *(Acts 6:9-7:1) —Flashcard 7.2*

4. **Stephen Answers the Accusations** *(Acts 7:2-53)*

5. **Stephen Is Stoned by the Crowd** *(Acts 7:54-60)*
    —Flashcard 7.3

Applying the Story
Stephen knew that even when people rejected him and meanly persecuted him, the Lord was always with him. He chose to be faithful to Jesus, and he never regretted it.

LESSON SEVEN
Stephen
Theme: Faithfulness

TEACHER'S CHECKLIST

- ❑ Read Acts 6:1–7, 60.
- ❑ Study Lesson Seven.
- ❑ Flash cards 7.1–7.3.
- ❑ Prepare snack—Heavenly Clouds.
- ❑ Gather for review game—small bag, review game letters from Ministry Resource download, small prizes for winners.
- ❑ Gather for object lesson—stuffed animal dog.
- ❑ Gather for craft—stickers, small containers, Bible verse printables from the Ministry Resource download.
- ❑ Print for teaching the memory verse—Memory Verse Flashcards and review game letters from the Ministry Resource download.
- ❑ Print for craft—Bible verse printables from the Ministry Resource download.
- ❑ Print and duplicate Coloring Pages or Activity Pages on the Ministry Resource download (one per student).
- ❑ Print and duplicate Take-Home Paper on the Ministry Resource download (one per student).

SCRIPTURES

Acts 6:1–7

1 And in those days, when the number of the disciples was multiplied, there arose a murmuring of the Grecians against the Hebrews, because their widows were neglected in the daily ministration.

2 Then the twelve called the multitude of the disciples unto them, and said, It is not reason that we should leave the word of God, and serve tables.

3 Wherefore, brethren, look ye out among you seven men of honest report, full of the Holy Ghost and wisdom, whom we may appoint over this business.

4 But we will give ourselves continually to prayer, and to the ministry of the word.

MEMORY VERSE

Luke 16:10a
"He that is faithful in that which is least is faithful also in much."

5 And the saying pleased the whole multitude: and they chose Stephen, a man full of faith and of the Holy Ghost, and Philip, and Prochorus, and Nicanor, and Timon, and Parmenas, and Nicolas a proselyte of Antioch:

6 Whom they set before the apostles: and when they had prayed, they laid their hands on them.

7 And the word of God increased; and the number of the disciples multiplied in Jerusalem greatly; and a great company of the priests were obedient to the faith.

BIBLE LESSON

Introducing the Story

The life of a Christian is full of more amazingly wonderful things than we could count, but let's see if we can list ten of these blessings. (Allow students to give ideas.)

- Christians are children of God—He is their Father.
- Christians know they will spend eternity (never-ending forever) in Heaven after they die.
- Christians get to actually know the God who created them and the world.
- Christians can have God's peace in their hearts.
- Christians know real love, because they know God, who is love.
- Christians can talk to God.
- Christians have the Bible to show them how to live God's way.
- Christians have their sins forgiven.
- Christians know they are accepted by God.
- Christians have the Holy Spirit living inside them.

We could name many more blessings of the Christian life. But not all parts of the Christian life are so easy and exciting—some parts we might not consider blessings at all.

Jesus—the One who made Christianity possible by His death to pay for our sins so we wouldn't have to pay for them ourselves, and His resurrection to give us eternal life—knew more about this less-than-easy part of the Christian life than any of us ever will. He told His followers (and that includes us) that all Christians will experience these circumstances.

John 15:18–20

18   If the world hate you, ye know that it hated me before it hated you.

19   If ye were of the world, the world would love his own: but because ye are not of the world, but I have chosen you out of the world, therefore the world hateth you.

20   Remember the word that I said unto you, The servant is not greater than his lord. If they have persecuted me, they will also persecute you; if they have kept my saying, they will keep yours also.

So, along with all the wonderful blessings of the Christian life, we will also experience what Jesus called the blessing of persecution. As hard as persecution may be (and it is hard), Jesus gave us a different perspective on it than we would ever have come up with on our own.

Matthew 5:10–12

10   Blessed are they which are persecuted for righteousness' sake: for theirs is the kingdom of heaven.

11   Blessed are ye, when men shall revile you, and persecute you, and shall say all manner of evil against you falsely, for my sake.

12   Rejoice, and be exceeding glad: for great is your reward in heaven: for so persecuted they the prophets which were before you.

The man in today's true story from the Bible suffered great persecution, and through it he was faithful to Jesus.

The Story

1. Stephen Chosen as a Deacon (Acts 6:1–5)

After Jesus died on the cross, many people believed in Him, and the church grew very quickly. Soon the church was so big that the disciples couldn't take care of all the needs of the church all by themselves.

"No one is taking care of some of the widows," some of the people complained. (These widows were women whose husbands had died, and they had no one to help care for their needs).

"Our job is to pray and to study the Bible so we can teach it to the people," the disciples answered. "We don't have enough time to do everything that needs to be done."

The disciples realized they needed help. "We need more leaders for the church," they said. "These men must be honest, and they must have good reputations. They must be wise, and they must be led by the Holy Spirit. If they have these qualities, they will be able to be leaders who are servants, which is just what we need."

Flash Card 7.1 ▶

All the people of the church searched for these Spirit-led, honest and wise men. When they found seven men who fit these qualifications, the disciples appointed these men to be servant-leaders over the church. These servant-leaders took care of the business of the church, such as making sure the widows had all their needs met; and the disciples continued to pray, study the Bible, and preach the Word of God to the people. Many, many more people heard the gospel and believed in Jesus Christ.

One of these faithful men chosen to be a servant-leader (in our church we call them deacons, which means servant) was Stephen.

2. Stephen Used of God (Acts 6:8)

Stephen did exactly what he was chosen to do. But Stephen had a burning desire in his heart to do even more. He was full of faith, and he was led by God's Holy Spirit.

Stephen was faithful. With all his heart, he wanted to bring glory to God. When God told him to do or say something, Stephen trusted God to enable him to do it or say it. God even used Stephen to do miracles that would show others God's greatness.

3. Stephen Brought into Questioning (Acts 6:9–7:1)

The Jewish religious leaders saw the miracles God performed through Stephen, and they heard Stephen give credit to Jesus for those miracles; and they became afraid. "If we allow this man to continue like this," the religious leaders said, "he will turn the Jews against our teachings. They will follow this Jesus whom Stephen teaches about."

The leaders went to Stephen. "Hey, what are you teaching our people? We teach them to follow the traditions of the Jews, and you teach something entirely different. You tell them they are sinners and need to trust Jesus for forgiveness. We don't like what you're saying."

But Stephen was faithful and walked in the power of the Holy Spirit; and he continued sharing the truth of God's Word. He taught that Jesus was God the Son. He taught that even though Moses (an early leader of the Israelites) had been a great leader through whom God had given the Jewish law, Jesus was greater than Moses. He taught that it is only through faith in Jesus—not through keeping the law or following the customs of the religious leaders—that we are saved.

The religious leaders knew deep in their hearts that Stephen was right. No matter how hard they tried to believe Stephen was lying, the Holy Spirit wouldn't let them. They knew Stephen spoke the wisdom of God.

Luke 21:15

15 For I will give you a mouth and wisdom, which all your adversaries shall not be able to gainsay nor resist.

"We need to get rid of this man," the religious leaders said. "But many of the people believe him. We have to turn the hearts of the people against him!"

The leaders knew exactly how to accomplish this—they would use lies. They found men who were willing to say under oath that they had heard Stephen speak against God and against Moses.

When the Jewish people heard these lies, they were furious. "What?! He's speaking against God and against Moses?" And they grabbed Stephen and brought him to the legal council.

The lies didn't stop there. The religious leaders arranged for more people to go to Stephen's trial and lie about him. "This man lies continually," these false witnesses accused. "He speaks lies against the temple and against the law God gave us. We even heard him say that this Jesus of Nazareth is going to destroy this temple and change the customs Moses brought to us from God!"

All the people turned toward Stephen, wondering what he could possibly answer for himself. But Stephen wasn't really thinking about his accusers. Right there, in the trial, Stephen was spending time with God, trusting Him to teach him what to say. In the middle of accusations, Stephen was walking with God in his heart. Stephen was faithful.

And when those people looked at Stephen, they saw the peace of God on his face—they "saw his face as it had been the face of an angel" (Acts 6:15).

"Are these accusations true?" the high priest asked Stephen.

TEACHER'S NOTE

dispute—to attempt to disprove by arguments or statements; to attempt to prove to be false, unfounded or erroneous; to attempt to overthrow by reasoning.

suborn—in law, to procure [obtain; persuade] a person to take such a false oath as constitutes perjury.

(Webster's 1828 Dictionary of the English Language)

Flash Card 7.2

TEACHER'S NOTE

These were the same accusations made against Jesus:

Matthew 26:59–61
"Now the chief priests, and elders, and all the council, sought false witness against Jesus, to put him to death; But found none: yea, though many false witnesses came, yet found they none. At the last came two false witnesses, 61 And said, This fellow said, I am able to destroy the temple of God, and to build it in three days."

---

4. Stephen Answers the Accusations (Acts 7:2–53)

Stephen knew the awful penalty for blasphemy (speaking lies) against God was stoning.

Leviticus 24:16

16 And he that blasphemeth the name of the LORD, he shall surely be put to death, and all the congregation shall certainly stone him: as well the stranger, as he that is born in the land, when he blasphemeth the name of the LORD, shall be put to death.

Stephen also knew he wasn't lying, but telling the truth according to God's Word. He knew, though, that the religious leaders didn't want to believe the truth, so they said he was lying. If Stephen would just say, "You know, I was wrong. What you guys are saying—follow the law and the Jewish customs, and you will go to heaven—is true. I agree with you," he would be allowed to go free.

But Stephen was faithful, and he trusted God. He wasn't afraid, and his faith in Jesus wouldn't let him deny the truth. "Listen to me," Stephen began, "we Jews have seen the God of glory work all through our history. He led Abraham, the father of our whole nation, to the land He promised to give him. God was with him, provided for him, and blessed him. And God was with Abraham's sons and grandsons and all his descendants that followed the Lord.

"When our people were made slaves in Egypt, God used Moses to deliver us from Egypt. Moses was faithful to God, and God was with Moses.

"But our people weren't faithful to God—they rejected Moses when they didn't like what he said. They gave up trusting in God, and in their hearts, they turned back to Egypt and the Egyptians' false gods.

"God sent many prophets to teach us the truth of His Word," Stephen continued. "They warned us to turn our hearts back to God. But our fathers persecuted and killed those prophets. Finally, God sent His Son, Jesus Christ, to be our Saviour from sin. But you, yourselves, have killed the Saviour, Jesus Christ!"

Flash Card 7.3

5. Stephen Is Stoned by the Crowd (Acts 7:54–60)

Stephen's words cut the people's hearts. The angry crowd couldn't stand to hear one more word, and they gnashed on him with their teeth.

Even in the middle of this angry mob, Stephen walked with God. Instead of looking at the faces of those hateful people who had lied about him and were even now persecuting him—Stephen looked up to heaven, the same place he had already been looking with his heart. God allowed faithful Stephen to see into heaven, and he saw Jesus! "I see the heavens opened, and the Son of man standing on the right hand of God" (Acts 7:56), Stephen proclaimed to all the people.

Only Stephen, who had been faithfully walking with God, saw this wonderful sight—the others saw only Stephen, and their own anger and bitterness. They plugged their ears and yelled as loud as they could, so they wouldn't have to hear Stephen's words anymore.

They threw Stephen out of the city, and they stoned him to death.

Even as he was being stoned, Stephen walked with God. He called to God, "I trust You, Lord Jesus. Receive my spirit." And he knelt down and cried out, "Lord, lay not this sin to their charge." And he died.

APPLYING THE STORY

I think we would agree that Stephen had great faith and that he suffered great persecution. He was lied about, and he was martyred (willingly suffered death rather than say he didn't believe what he really believed) for his beliefs. Although he knew he would likely be stoned to death because the religious leaders called the truth that he taught lies, Stephen was still faithful. He was full of faith that God was right and good and that he could trust Him, even though Stephen didn't know what would happen to him.

Proverbs 3:5–6

5   Trust in the LORD with all thine heart; and lean not unto thine own understanding.

6   In all thy ways acknowledge him, and he shall direct thy paths.

This was not the first time Stephen was found faithful or that his faith was tested. Stephen had shown himself faithful so often throughout his life that all the people knew him as a man full of faith.

Acts 6:5a

5a And the saying pleased the whole multitude; and they chose Stephen, a man full of faith and of the Holy Ghost...

TEACHER'S NOTE

If students share that they are having problems at home because they are Christians, you could encourage them to trust the Lord and to honor Him through honoring their parents.

Ephesians 6:2 *"Honour thy father and mother; (which is the first commandment with promise;)"*

You see, persecution doesn't only come to us in big frightening ways, as came to Stephen in this true story.

- You may be laughed at, called names, or be rejected by your friends because you believe in Jesus.

- You may be laughed at for bringing your Bible to school.

- You may be mocked for standing alone and not participating in an activity that is against God's Word.

- You may be bullied for your beliefs. (Someone may take your lunch or even hit you.)

- You may be lied about.

- If your parents are not Christians, they may ridicule you or not allow you to go to church.

- Someone may put up ugly posts about you on Facebook.

These are likely the kinds of things that happened to Stephen in the beginning:

- Someone may have made fun of him or called him names to try to make him feel worthless, or his friends may have said they didn't want anything to do with him because he believed in Jesus; but still he was faithful to Jesus.

- Someone may have told him he couldn't share the gospel, but he was faithful to Jesus and shared it anyway.

- He may have been attacked for going to church, but still he was faithful and continued to go to church.

- Someone may have shoved him or hit him because he believed in Jesus; but still he was faithful to Jesus.

- Someone may have lied about him; but he continued to be faithful to Jesus.

- His family may have rejected him, but still he was faithful to Jesus.

Stephen couldn't have remained faithful through all of this on his own, and neither can you. Stephen could only be "full of faith" because he was "full of the Holy Ghost" (Acts 6:3).

Remember our lesson about Peter? Peter was also "full of the Holy Ghost," because he chose to trust God:

- Peter chose to walk by God's commands, instead of choosing the comfortable path. (Galatians 5:16, 25)

- Peter chose not to live in ways that are against God's instructions in the Bible (anger, immorality, dishonesty, stealing, ungodly lifestyle and speech, etc.). (Ephesians 4:1–32)

- Peter chose to follow the Holy Spirit's leading in his life. (1 Thessalonians 5:19)

- Peter chose not to trust the wisdom of man, but to trust in the power of the Holy Spirit. (1 Corinthians 2:5)

Like Peter, Stephen made these same choices. And he chose, through the strength of the Holy Spirit, to walk by faith.

Every time Stephen chose to be faithful to Jesus, God strengthened him and gave him courage for the next time.

Psalm 27:14

14 Wait on the LORD: be of good courage, and he shall strengthen thine heart: wait, I say, on the LORD.

He stood up to lies and ridicule, and the Lord strengthened him.

Isaiah 41:10

10 Fear thou not; for I am with thee: be not dismayed; for I am thy God: I will strengthen thee; yea, I will help thee; yea, I will uphold thee with the right hand of my righteousness.

If someone tried to get him to sin against God, he stood alone and did right; and the Lord strengthened him.

1 Peter 5:10

10 But the God of all grace, who hath called us unto his eternal glory by Christ Jesus, after that ye have suffered a while, make you perfect, stablish, strengthen, settle you.

His "friends" threatened to reject him if he didn't change his beliefs, but he loved Jesus more than their approval, and the Lord strengthened him.

Ephesians 6:10

10 Finally, my brethren, be strong in the Lord, and in the power of his might.

Stephen knew that no matter who rejected him or what they did to him, the Lord was always with him. He chose to be faithful to Jesus, and he never regretted it.

Hebrews 13:5b

5 ...for he hath said, I will never leave thee, nor forsake thee.

REVIEW GAME/QUESTIONS

Materials Needed

Small bag

Review game printables from Ministry Resource download (circles containing letters to spell faithful or faithfulness, plus x's)

Small prizes for winners

Set Up

Cut the circle game pieces and place in a small bag.

Playing the Game

Ask the students questions from the list below. When a student answers correctly, allow him to come to the front and draw a letter from the bag.

This game is played teacher vs. student and the goal for the students is to spell the word faithful (or faithfulness, depending on the time you have to play the game) before drawing three X's from the bag. If the students can do this, the entire class receives a small treat.

1. What is the term for cruel or painful treatment because a person believes in Jesus? (Note: Jesus called this a blessing.)
    Answer: Persecution

2. What were the responsibilities of the servant leaders in the church?
    Answer: They took care of the business of the church, such as caring for the widows.

3. What was the name of the man in our story who was chosen to be a servant-leader, or deacon?
    Answer: Stephen

4. What plan did the religious leaders come up with to get rid of Stephen?
   Answer: They would find people to tell lies about Stephen.

5. What crime did the Jewish religious leaders accuse Stephen of?
   Answer: Lying and blasphemy

6. What was the punishment for blasphemy?
   Answer: Stoning

7. Did Stephen lie about God?
   Answer: No. Stephen taught the truth of God's Word.

8. Where did Stephen look, and whom did he see, while he was being persecuted?
   Answer: He looked toward heaven and he saw Jesus.

9. Stephen was not only full of faith, but he was also full of _____?
   Answer: The Holy Spirit

10. What did God do for Stephen (and for us!) each time he chose to be faithful to God?
    Answer: He strengthened him.

Teaching the Memory Verse

Luke 16:10a
10 He that is faithful in that which is least is faithful also in much:

Materials Needed
Memory Verse Flashcards from Ministry Resource download
Review game letters from the Ministry Resource download

Teaching the Verse
Use the same bag of letters from the review game, removing the three X's. Write the verse on the board, and ask your class to recite it together one time. Then, allow a student to pick a letter from the bag and erase all matching letters off the verse on the board. (For instance, if a student draws the letter, A, he may erase all the a's found in the memory verse.) Have the class say the verse again with the missing letters. Repeat this process until no letters remain in the bag.

OBJECT LESSON—Faithful Friend

Materials Needed

Stuffed Animal Dog

(If your classroom setting and student conditions and ages are conducive to this type of object lesson, consider bringing a small dog in a crate or carrier.)

Lesson

They say that a dog is man's best friend! How many of you have a dog or even a couple dogs at home? Do you enjoy playing with them? What are some ways you would describe your dog? (Allow for feedback.)

Does anyone in this class have a dog that follows you everywhere—one that is always by your side?

Application

Dogs are known for being faithful to their owners. Today, we learned about a hero in the Bible who was faithful to his Master. Stephen was faithful to God. Even when others bit him and threw rocks at him, Stephen loved God and prayed to Him. Stephen was faithful to God until the day that he died. Let's live like Stephen this week—and for the rest of our lives! Faithful to Jesus until death, no matter what comes into our lives. And, let's thank Jesus for always being loyal and faithful to us.

CRAFT—Faithfulness Containers

Supplies

Stickers

Small containers (one per student)

Bible verse printables from the Ministry Resource download

Instructions

1. Print and cut the Bible verse printables.
2. Give each student a small container, stickers, and the Bible verse printables.
3. Instruct the students to decorate the container with stickers. Insert the Bible verses into the container.

Application

Encourage your class to choose one Bible verse each day and memorize it. Hiding God's Word in their hearts will help each student to develop a love for God and a desire to remain faithful to Him day by day.

ADDITIONAL RESOURCES

Find the following items on the Ministry Resource download:

- Coloring Page (for younger children)
- Activity Page (for older children)
- Student Take-Home Paper
- PowerPoint Presentation

Suggested Classroom Schedule

Before Class		Complete attendance record. Provide students with coloring pages/activity pages.
Opening		Welcome
Prayer		Prayer requests and praise reports from the children
Song Time		
Memory Verse		Psalm 96:3
Song Time		
Object Lesson		Obeying Instructions
Bible Lesson		Philip
Application/Invitation		Help saved students apply lesson. Invite unsaved students to receive Christ.
Snack		Scripture Cookies
Review Game/ Questions		
Craft		Salvation Cards
Closing		Give announcements and pray. Distribute take-home papers.

Lesson Eight Overview

Philip
Theme—Readiness to Share the Gospel

Scripture
Acts 6:1-7

Memory Verse
Psalm 96:3— "*Declare his glory among the heathen, his wonders among all people.*"

Lesson Outline
Introducing the Story
Telling others about Jesus and His death on the cross to pay for their sins is a job God has given to every Christian. The man in our true story from the Bible decided he would always be ready to share the gospel (good news of Jesus Christ) wherever he went.

Telling the Story
1. **Philip Chosen as a Deacon** (*Acts 6:1-5*)
2. **Philip Preaches God's Word** (*Acts 8:4-25*)
3. **An Angel Sends Philip to the Desert** (*Acts 8:26-27*) —*Flashcard 8.1*
4. **Philip Meets the Ethiopian** (*Acts 8:27-31*) —*Flashcard 8.2*
5. **Philip Preaches Jesus to the Ethiopian** (*Acts 8:32-35*)
6. **The Ethiopian Believes and Is Baptized** (*Acts 8:36-39*) —*Flashcard 8.3*

Applying the Story
Whatever job or occupation you have in life, always remember that the very most important job you have is to share the gospel with others. Study, pray, obey the Holy Spirit, and go where He leads you and be ready to share the gospel.

LESSON EIGHT

8 Philip

Theme: Readiness to Share the Gospel

TEACHER'S CHECKLIST

- ❑ Read Acts 6:1–7; 8:26–40.
- ❑ Study Lesson Eight.
- ❑ Flash cards 8.1–8.3.
- ❑ Prepare snack—Scripture Cookies.
- ❑ Gather for "Use an Object"—occupation props.
- ❑ Gather for object lesson—cupcakes, 2 boxes of cake mix, ingredients needed for cake mix (oil, egg, water), mixing bowl and spoon, motor oil, additional egg, glass of dirty water.
- ❑ Gather for craft—binder clips, printable salvation cards from the Ministry Resource download, white card stock.
- ❑ Gather for teaching the memory verse—Memory Verse Flashcards and *Are You Smarter Than a Fifth Grader* PowerPoint game from the Ministry Resource download, dry-erase marker and board.
- ❑ Print for review game—occupation cards from the Ministry Resource download.
- ❑ Print Memory Verse Flashcards from the Ministry Resource download.
- ❑ Print for craft—printable salvation cards from the Ministry Resource download.
- ❑ Print and duplicate Coloring Pages or Activity Pages on the Ministry Resource download (one per student).
- ❑ Print and duplicate Take-Home Paper on the Ministry Resource download (one per student).

SCRIPTURES

Acts 6:1–7

1 And in those days, when the number of the disciples was multiplied, there arose a murmuring of the Grecians against the Hebrews, because their widows were neglected in the daily ministration.

SNACK SUGGESTION

Scripture Cookies
Purchase Fig Newtons and trim off one long side with a sharp knife, to match the shape of a book and to give three edges a paper-like look, with the binding on the fourth, left-side edge.

Cut small pieces of red Fruit Roll-Ups in the shape of a bookmark, and insert into the middle of the Fig Newton with the help of a toothpick.

Decorate the Bible by piping white icing around the edges and a cross in the middle.

Explain that the Ethiopian man was searching the Scriptures, trying to learn more about Jesus, and that Philip was ready to share the truth of the Gospel to him, because he obeyed God's command to go to the desert.

MEMORY VERSE

Psalm 96:3
"Declare his glory among the heathen, his wonders among all people."

2 Then the twelve called the multitude of the disciples unto them, and said, It is not reason that we should leave the word of God, and serve tables.

3 Wherefore, brethren, look ye out among you seven men of honest report, full of the Holy Ghost and wisdom, whom we may appoint over this business.

4 But we will give ourselves continually to prayer, and to the ministry of the word.

5 And the saying pleased the whole multitude: and they chose Stephen, a man full of faith and of the Holy Ghost, and Philip, and Prochorus, and Nicanor, and Timon, and Parmenas, and Nicolas a proselyte of Antioch:

6 Whom they set before the apostles: and when they had prayed, they laid their hands on them.

7 And the word of God increased; and the number of the disciples multiplied in Jerusalem greatly; and a great company of the priests were obedient to the faith.

BIBLE LESSON

Introducing the Story

USE AN OBJECT

For each of the occupation examples (or for any of your own), consider bringing a corresponding prop for each, allowing a student to stand in front of the class with the prop while you teach the introduction to the lesson.

Who can tell me what the word *occupation* means? An occupation is the name for the type of work a person does. For instance, a doctor who takes care of animals has what occupation? (veterinarian) A person who flies an airplane has what occupation? (pilot) A person who makes bread, pies, cookies, and rolls to sell has what occupation? (baker) A person who arranges flowers and plants and sells them has what occupation? (florist) A person who works in a library has what occupation? (librarian)

What occupation does your mom or dad have? (Allow students to give brief answers.)

I have one final question: A person who tells people about Jesus and how they can have their sins forgiven has what occupation? (Answers may vary, but will likely include pastor, missionary, or Sunday school teacher.)

Pastors and Sunday school teachers do have the special responsibility of teaching others about Jesus, but God's Word teaches that it is not a special job for only a few people. Telling others about Jesus and His death on the cross to pay for their sins is a job God has given to every Christian.

Psalm 96:3

3 Declare his glory among the heathen, his wonders among all people.

Matthew 28:19–20

19 Go ye therefore, and teach all nations, baptizing them in the name of the Father, and of the Son, and of the Holy Ghost:

20 Teaching them to observe all things whatsoever I have commanded you: and, lo, I am with you alway, even unto the end of the world. Amen.

The man in our true story from the Bible decided he would always be ready to share the gospel (good news of Jesus Christ) wherever he went.

TEACHER'S NOTE

A student may point out that this command in Matthew 28 was given to the disciples, which is true. Note, however, that Jesus said, "teaching them to observe all things whatsoever I have commanded you," (which would include going, teaching, etc.). If the command was, in fact, only intended for the disciples, they were to teach everyone else to share the gospel, just as Jesus had taught them. The command, therefore, includes everyone.

The Story

1. Philip Chosen as a Deacon (Acts 6:1–5)

Last week we learned that seven men were chosen to be servant-leaders, or deacons to serve in the church at Jerusalem. The job of these servant-leaders was to take care of the business of the church, including caring for the widows. This would give the disciples, who were the preachers, more time to do what they really needed to do—pray and study the Bible so they could teach it to the people.

All the people of the church searched for men who met the qualifications given to them by the disciples—honest, good reputations, wise, and led by the Spirit of God.

When they found seven men who met the qualifications, the disciples appointed these seven to be servant-leaders over the church. With the help of these servant-leaders, many more people were able to hear the gospel and believe in Jesus Christ.

2. Philip Preaches God's Word (Acts 8:4–25)

Not everyone in Jerusalem liked the Christians. Many of the religious leaders were jealous of people following Jesus, and they persecuted Christians. They beat Christians, put Christians in prison, and even killed Christians.

"We've got to get out of here," many of the Christians said. "We need to go to other places and share the gospel, so everyone can hear and have a chance to believe in Jesus. If we don't leave right away, we will be killed, and we will not have the opportunity to tell other people about the Lord Jesus Christ."

One of the Christians who quickly left Jerusalem so he could preach the gospel was Philip, one of the servant-leaders. Philip wasn't one of Jesus' twelve disciples whose primary job was to preach to all the people, but he realized it was everyone's job to preach. Philip shared the good news of Jesus Christ wherever he went. He preached in the city of Samaria, where many people believed in Jesus after they heard Philip preach and saw that Philip truly knew God. The people who trusted Jesus were filled with great joy.

Acts 8:8
8   And there was great joy in that city.

3. An Angel Sends Philip to the Desert (Acts 8:26–27)

Flash Card 8.1

Philip continued preaching the gospel in other villages (Acts 8:25), and one day, as Philip was serving the Lord, an angel came to him. Philip had always followed the Lord's directions so closely, and he knew the Lord so well, that he wasn't afraid when he saw the angel. "Go south into the Gaza desert," the angel instructed.

"I'll go," thought Philip. "Strange that God would send me into the desert, when there are so many people right here I can share the gospel with." He immediately got up and went where the angel told him to go.

Acts 8:27a
27   And he arose and went:

4. Philip Meets the Ethiopian (Acts 8:27–31)

"I wonder why the Lord is sending me to the desert," Philip wondered as he journeyed.

Then, way off in the distance, he saw a chariot. In the chariot was a wealthy man from Ethiopia—the treasurer of all the money of the queen of Ethiopia. This very important Ethiopian man was on his way back from Jerusalem, where he had gone to worship God. He didn't yet know about Jesus, but he wanted to learn all he could about God, so he read the Bible as he traveled home.

"Go to that chariot, and speak to that man," the Spirit of the Lord instructed Philip. "Now, this is exciting!" thought Philip. "Maybe I will be able to tell this man about Jesus!"

Flash Card 8.2

When Philip came near, he heard the Ethiopian man reading Isaiah 53 from the Bible. "He's reading the Bible," thought Philip. "God truly has prepared this man's heart to hear the gospel." He spoke to the man, "Excuse me, sir, do you understand what that passage means?"

"Now, how can I understand it unless someone teaches it to me?" the man asked. Then he looked at Philip with pleading eyes. "Would you be willing to come sit by me and explain it to me?"

"So this is why the angel sent me to the desert. This is why the Spirit of God told me to speak to this wealthy man in the chariot," Philip thought as he climbed up and sat next to the man. "I have the opportunity to tell this man about my Saviour, the Lord Jesus Christ! Hooray—I love the desert!"

And right there, in a chariot in the middle of the desert, Philip taught the Ethiopian man about Jesus.

5. Philip Preaches Jesus to the Ethiopian (Acts 8:32–35)

"I don't understand those verses," the Ethiopian said as he finished reading a passage out loud.

Isaiah 53:7–8

7 He was oppressed, and he was afflicted, yet he opened not his mouth: he is brought as a lamb to the slaughter, and as a sheep before her shearers is dumb, so he openeth not his mouth.

8 He was taken from prison and from judgment: and who shall declare his generation? for he was cut off out of the land of the living: for the transgression of my people was he stricken.

"When the prophet Isaiah wrote this, was he talking about himself, or was he talking about somebody else?"

"Sir, he was talking about the Messiah, the Saviour from sin, for Whom all the Israelites have been waiting for hundreds of years. That Messiah has come.

"This tells us that Jesus Christ (the Messiah) died—that He was led to the cross like a sheep to be killed as a sacrifice. The Messiah has come, and He suffered ("He was oppressed, and He was afflicted") without a word of complaint ("yet He opened not His mouth")—for us on the cross ("for the transgression of my people was He stricken")."

"God is so kind to use me, allowing me to share the gospel with this man," Philip thought. "I'm so thankful I have studied the Bible so I know how to answer the man's questions. There is nothing more important in the whole world than sharing the gospel. I would rather tell people about Jesus than do anything else in the whole world!"

Deuteronomy 6:6–9

6 And these words, which I command thee this day, shall be in thine heart:

> **TEACHER'S NOTE**
>
> You may wish to briefly explain the purpose of Old Testament sacrifices:
>
> The animals that were sacrificed before the Messiah came were symbols of what Jesus would do for us on the cross. The animals were sacrificed to remind people that the price of sin was death and that "without shedding of blood is no remission," (Hebrews 9:22b)

7   And thou shalt teach them diligently unto thy children, and shalt talk of them when thou sittest in thine house, and when thou walkest by the way, and when thou liest down, and when thou risest up.

8   And thou shalt bind them for a sign upon thine hand, and they shall be as frontlets between thine eyes.

9   And thou shalt write them upon the posts of thy house, and on thy gates.

Job 23:12b

12   ...I have esteemed the words of his mouth more than my necessary food.

Psalm 1:2

2   But his delight is in the law of the LORD; and in his law doth he meditate day and night.

Flash Card 8.3

TEACHER'S NOTE

You may wish to share that baptism is just a picture that we have been saved, not part of salvation itself. The Ethiopian man wanted to be baptized to identify with Christ, because he was already saved, not because he wanted to become saved.

Just as a wedding ring shows others that we are married (it doesn't make us married), baptism shows others that we are saved (it doesn't make us saved.)

6. The Ethiopian Believes and Is Baptized (Acts 8:36–39)

The Ethiopian man believed what Philip told him. "Lord, I believe in You," he spoke quietly in his heart to the Lord. "You are the Messiah Who died for my sins, and Who rose again from the dead. I believe!"

"Hey, look here!" the Ethiopian man called out excitedly. "Here is water—is there any reason I can't be baptized?"

"Do you believe with all your heart?" Philip asked.

"I sure do. I believe that Jesus is the Son of God—the Messiah Who has come to pay the price for my sins. Yes, I believe!"

"Stop the chariot," Philip called to the driver. And Philip and the Ethiopian man got out, waded into the water, and Philip baptized the Ethiopian right there, in the middle of the desert.

"It's so wonderful to be a Christian," thought the Ethiopian man, as he shook himself to dry off a little. "Hey, Philip, thank you for…" he began, but Philip was gone. "Thank You, Lord, for sending that man to share the gospel with me," the Ethiopian prayed. "I've never been so happy in my life!"

Acts 8:39

39   And when they were come up out of the water, the Spirit of the Lord caught away Philip, that the eunuch saw him no more: and he went on his way rejoicing.

APPLYING THE STORY

What if Philip had thought, "I am not a pastor. My occupation is a servant leader. My job is to take care of the business matters of the church. My job is to help the widows—it's not my job to tell people about Jesus—that's the pastor's job."

What would have happened to Philip if he had stayed? The church at Jerusalem scattered, going to many different places. There would have been no church for Philip to serve in anymore. Philip would have thought, "I don't have any job to do now." He would have felt useless.

What would have happened to the people in Samaria and the other towns where Philip went? If he hadn't studied God's Word, and if he hadn't had a heart to share the gospel with others, who would have preached to those people? What if he had thought, "That's not my job. A pastor needs to come here and tell the people about Jesus."

What would have happened to the Ethiopian man? What if Philip had said, "You know, I don't really know that much about the Bible. I hope you can meet a pastor sometime. A pastor could tell you all about the Bible. It's a pastor's job—not mine."

What if God sent you into the desert? Would you go? What if God told you to speak to the Ethiopian man? Would you do it?

If you did speak to the Ethiopian man, what would you say? Do you know what the Bible says about forgiveness of sins through Jesus' death, burial, and resurrection? Do you know how to lead someone to Jesus? Or have you never thought of it as your job?

2 Timothy 2:15

15 Study to shew thyself approved unto God, a workman that needeth not to be ashamed, rightly dividing the word of truth.

The truth is, God has sent us many places. Maybe it has never been into the desert like it was for Philip. Maybe God has sent you to your grandparents' house, or your cousins' house, where your relatives don't know Jesus Christ as their Saviour.

Maybe He has sent you to a school, where your classmates and teachers don't know Jesus Christ as their Saviour.

Maybe He has sent you to the park, where other children playing there don't know Jesus Christ as their Saviour.

Maybe He has sent you to your own home, where your parents or brothers or sisters don't know Jesus Christ as their Saviour.

Wherever we are, that is the place God wants us to share the gospel. He wants sharing the gospel to be the strongest desire of our lives, like it was for Philip. He wants us to be prepared to share the gospel, like Philip was. He wants us to go where He sends us, like Philip did.

What are some ways you can be sure you are ready to share the gospel wherever and whenever God leads you? (Allow response.)

- If you obey your parents in daily life, you will be prepared to obey the Holy Spirit when He leads you in your heart to share the gospel with someone.

Luke 16:10

10 He that is faithful in that which is least is faithful also in much: and he that is unjust in the least is unjust also in much.

- If you carry tracts with you, you will always be able to leave the gospel for someone to read, even if you aren't able to tell the gospel at the time.

- If you memorize verses that teach how to trust Jesus as Saviour, you will always be prepared with God's Word hidden in your heart.

- If you read the Bible every day, you will grow to know more about God and to know Him better, so you will want to talk about Him.

- If you follow the leading of the Holy Spirit when He encourages you in your heart to speak to a particular person about the Lord, you will grow in boldness to share the gospel.

- If you thank God often for your salvation, and you think of your own testimony of how you trusted Christ, it will be fresh in your mind so you can share it with others.

- If you pray for the opportunity to share the gospel with others, God will give opportunities to you, just like He gave to Philip.

Whatever job or occupation you have in life, always remember that the very most important job you have is to share the gospel with others. Then study, pray, obey the Holy Spirit, and go where He leads you and be ready to share the gospel.

TEACHER'S TIP

You may want to give each student a supply of tracts from your church, encouraging them to carry them with them and be prepared to give them out throughout the week.

Be sure to ask for testimonies next week in relation to this activity!

TEACHER'S TIP

As time permits, ask students to share their salvation testimonies, and give them tips on how to include their testimony in a gospel presentation.

REVIEW GAME/QUESTIONS

Materials Needed

Occupation cards from the Ministry Resource Download

Set Up

Arrange occupation cards on a pocket chart or tape them to the board.

Playing the Game

Divide the class into two teams, and explain that the object of this game is to spell the word, GOSPEL.

Ask a question to Team One, and if the student answers correctly, allow him to come to the board and pick an occupation. Turn the card over to show the letter, and arrange it at the top of the board or pocket chart. Follow the same instructions for Team Two and alternate until a team has successfully spelled the word, GOSPEL.

The first team to complete the challenge wins the game.

Remind students that no matter what occupation they may have when they are older, they can always share the Gospel with others, just like Philip did.

1. Why did Philip leave Jerusalem?
    Answer: The Christians were being persecuted—beaten, imprisoned, and some were put to death.

2. What was Philip doing when the angel came to him?
    Answer: Serving the Lord; preaching

3. Where did God send Philip?
    Answer: To the desert

4. What was the Ethiopian man's job?
    Answer: He was the treasurer of all the queen's money.

5. What did the Ethiopian man want to do as soon as he believed in Jesus?
    Answer: He wanted to be baptized.

6. What happened to Philip after he baptized the man?
    Answer: The Spirit of the Lord caught him away.

7. What are some places God has sent you to tell others about Him? \
    Answer: Answers will vary.

8. Who did God give the responsibility of telling others about Jesus and how they can have their sins forgiven too?
   Answer: Every Christian

9. What are some ways you can be sure you are ready to share the gospel wherever and whenever God leads you?
   Answer: Answers will vary, but should include: carrying tracts, memorizing Bible verses, praying for opportunity, etc.

10. What is the very most important job we have?
    Answer: To share the gospel with others

Teaching the Memory Verse

Psalm 96:3

3 Declare his glory among the heathen, his wonders among all people.

Materials Needed

Memory Verse Flashcards from the Ministry Resource download
Are You Smarter Than a Fifth Grader PowerPoint game from the Ministry Resource download
Dry Erase marker and board

Teaching the Verse

In this modified version of Are You Smarter Than a Fifth Grader, call on one student to complete each challenge, allowing the class to help if needed. After each challenge is completed, ask the class to recite the verse together.

THIRD GRADE

Spelling: Spell the missing word in the verse.
Declare his glory among the _____, his wonders among all people.

Art: Draw the missing word on the board.
Declare his glory among the heathen, his wonders among all _____.

Math: On the board, add the first two numbers in the reference.
Psalm 96:3

Penmanship: Write the missing word on the board.

Declare his glory _____ the heathen, his wonders among all people.

FOURTH GRADE

Spelling: Spell the missing word in the verse.

Declare his glory among the heathen, his _____ among all people.

Art: Draw the missing word on the board.

_____ his glory among the heathen, his wonders among all people.

Math: On the board, multiply the first two numbers in the reference.

Psalm 96:3

Penmanship: Write the missing word on the board.

Declare his glory among the heathen, his wonders among all _____.

FIFTH GRADE

Spelling: Spell the missing word in the verse.

Declare his glory among the _____, his wonders among all people.

Art: Draw the missing word on the board.

Declare his _____ among the heathen, his wonders among all people.

Math: On the board, write the numbers from the reference in order. Now, add mathematical symbols to make the statement true.

9−6=3

Penmanship: Write the missing words on the board.

_____ _____ _____ among the heathen, his wonders among all people.

OBJECT LESSON
—Obeying Instructions

Materials Needed

Cupcakes (prepared before class)
2 boxes of cake mix
Ingredients needed for cake mix (oil, egg, water)
Mixing bowl and spoon
Motor oil
Additional egg
Glass of dirty water

Lesson

At the front of the class, set up a table for a baking demonstration, placing the ingredients where the students can watch you prepare the cupcakes.

Tell the students that you are so excited to bake cupcakes today, and that you are going to demonstrate the preparation by following the instructions listed on the cake box mix. Continue to introduce the baking demonstration by talking about how much you love to bake and especially love to lick the bowl after you've mixed the cake batter. (Allow for feedback and interaction with the students.)

Proceed to prepare the cupcakes as directed on the package, but replace cooking oil with motor oil. Then, crack the egg, dumping the entire egg and shell into the bowl. Finally, replace a measuring cup of clean water with a glass of dirty water.

For each ingredient, pause to allow feedback and reaction from your students. Perhaps even exaggerate your motions and confidence in baking the cupcakes.

After preparing a batch of cupcakes incorrectly, start over, this time following the instructions clearly and calmly and using the right ingredients as listed on the cake mix box.

Application

What was my problem the first time I prepared a batch of cupcake batter? I didn't follow the instructions carefully. I did my own thing and wasn't ready with the right ingredients for preparing delicious cupcakes. The second time, I was ready to carefully obey the instructions listed on the box. And, because I was ready and willing to obey, look at the beautiful cupcakes that can be a result! (Show the cupcakes you prepared before class.)

Jesus had a special job for Philip, and Philip was able to lead the Ethiopian man to the Lord because he followed God's instructions to go to the desert. He was willing and ready to share the Gospel with others. This week, follow God's instructions to you to be ready to share your faith with those God brings to your path!

Note: As an alternate snack option, consider serving the prepared cupcakes to your students.

CRAFT—Salvation Cards

Supplies

Binder clips
Printable salvation cards from Ministry
Resource download
White card stock

Instructions

1. Print off a set of salvation cards and cut into small cards.
2. Give each student a set of salvation cards and a binder clip.
3. Have the students put the binder clip on the cards and set upright.

Application

Encourage the students to be ready to share the gospel by memorizing the verses and sharing them with someone who does not know Jesus as Saviour.

ADDITIONAL RESOURCES

Find the following items on the Ministry Resource download:

- Coloring Page (for younger children)
- Activity Page (for older children)
- Student Take-Home Paper
- PowerPoint Presentation

Suggested Classroom Schedule

Before Class	Complete attendance record. Provide students with coloring pages/activity pages.
Opening	Welcome
Prayer	Prayer requests and praise reports from the children
Song Time	
Memory Verse	Proverbs 12:22
Song Time	
Object Lesson	Covering Lies
Bible Lesson	Ananias and Sapphira
Application/Invitation	Help saved students apply lesson. Invite unsaved students to receive Christ.
Snack	100 Grand or Carrot Coins
Review Game/ Questions	
Craft	What Is Hiding in Your Heart?
Closing	Give announcements and pray. Distribute take-home papers.

Lesson Nine Overview

Ananias and Sapphira

Theme—Truthfulness

Scripture

Acts 5:1-11

Memory Verse

Proverbs 12:22—*"Lying lips are abomination to the LORD: but they that deal truly are his delight."*

Lesson Outline

Introducing the Story

Truth is very important to God. Everything about God is truth. In fact, Jesus, God the Son, called Himself the Truth. Today's true story from the Bible is about a man named Ananias and his wife Sapphira, and from their lives, we can learn the importance of telling the truth.

Telling the Story

1. **Church Members Give** *(Acts 4:32–37)*
   —*Flashcard 9.1*

2. **Ananias and Sapphira Make a Plan**
   (Acts 5:2; 9a) —*Flashcard 9.2*

3. **Ananias Lies to the Holy Spirit** *(Acts 5:1–6)*

4. **Sapphira Lies** *(Acts 5:7–10)*
   —*Flashcard 9.3*

5. **The Church Fears God** *(Acts 5:11)*

Applying the Story

Speaking lies is such a sad thing in a Christian's life. When a Christian is untruthful, it is because they are not believing the truthfulness of God; but God is always truthful. Man lies, but God never does.

9 LESSON NINE
Ananias and Sapphira
Theme: Truthfulness

TEACHER'S CHECKLIST

- ☐ Read Acts 4:32–5:11.
- ☐ Study Lesson Nine.
- ☐ Flash cards 9.1–9.3.
- ☐ Prepare snack—100 Grand candy bars or Carrot Coins.
- ☐ Gather for "Use an Object"—picture cards from the Ministry Resource download, poster board, Crayola Color Switchers markers.
- ☐ Gather for review game—True/False cards from the Ministry Resource download, clothespins.
- ☐ Gather for teaching the verse—Memory Verse Flashcards from the Ministry Resource download, lemon wedges, and Tootsie Pops.
- ☐ Gather for object lesson—glass jar filled halfway with water, one quarter, pennies (one per student).
- ☐ Gather for craft—Ananias & Sapphira Puzzle from the Ministry Resource download, children's scissors, crayons, heart-shaped box or container.
- ☐ Print for "Use an Object"—picture cards from the Ministry Resource download.
- ☐ Print for review game—True/False cards from the Ministry Resource download.
- ☐ Print Memory Verse Flashcards from the Ministry Resource download.
- ☐ Print for craft—Ananias & Sapphira Puzzle printable from the Ministry Resource download.
- ☐ Print and duplicate Coloring Pages or Activity Pages on the Ministry Resource download (one per student).
- ☐ Print and duplicate Take-Home Paper on the Ministry Resource download (one per student).

SNACK SUGGESTION

100 Grand Candy Bars or Carrot Coins

Serve 100 Grand candy bars and discuss the fact that Ananias and Sapphira stole money from the Lord. For a healthier variation, slice carrots into small discs and serve "Carrot Coins."

MEMORY VERSE

Proverbs 12:22
"Lying lips are abomination to the LORD: but they that deal truly are his delight."

SCRIPTURES

Acts 5:1–11

1   But a certain man named Ananias, with Sapphira his wife, sold a possession,

2   And kept back part of the price, his wife also being privy to it, and brought a certain part, and laid it at the apostles' feet.

3   But Peter said, Ananias, why hath Satan filled thine heart to lie to the Holy Ghost, and to keep back part of the price of the land?

4   Whiles it remained, was it not thine own? and after it was sold, was it not in thine own power? why hast thou conceived this thing in thine heart? thou hast not lied unto men, but unto God.

5   And Ananias hearing these words fell down, and gave up the ghost: and great fear came on all them that heard these things.

6   And the young men arose, wound him up, and carried him out, and buried him.

7   And it was about the space of three hours after, when his wife, not knowing what was done, came in.

8   And Peter answered unto her, Tell me whether ye sold the land for so much? And she said, Yea, for so much.

9   Then Peter said unto her, How is it that ye have agreed together to tempt the Spirit of the Lord? behold, the feet of them which have buried thy husband are at the door, and shall carry thee out.

10   Then fell she down straightway at his feet, and yielded up the ghost: and the young men came in, and found her dead, and, carrying her forth, buried her by her husband.

11   And great fear came upon all the church, and upon as many as heard these things.

BIBLE LESSON

Introducing the Story

Have you ever heard of a "little white lie"? That's the term people sometimes give to lies that don't seem that bad or important to them.

Can you think of lies that people might consider "little white lies"? (Allow response.)

- Telling your mom your room is clean when really you stuffed clean clothes into the corners of your closet

- Telling your mom you didn't eat any of the cookies sitting on the counter, when you really did

- Letting your dad think someone else spilled juice on his letter, when it was actually you

- Telling your teacher you lost your homework, when the truth is, you didn't complete it

If these are little white lies, what is it that would classify a lie as a really bad lie? (Allow response.)

- If it is something that results in an injury to someone?

- If it gets someone else in serious trouble?

- If it hurts you?

A lie is anything that isn't true—big or little. There is no such thing as a little white lie, or a lie that doesn't matter.

What is the opposite of a lie called? (Allow response.) The opposite of a lie is the truth.

Truth is very important to God. Everything about God is truth. In fact, Jesus, God the Son, called Himself the Truth.

John 14:6

6   Jesus saith unto him, I am the way, the truth, and the life: no man cometh unto the Father, but by me.

Truth is so much a part of God, that when we speak truth, it's not just okay with God—it thrills Him.

Proverbs 12:22

22   Lying lips are abomination to the LORD: but they that deal truly are his delight.

We don't just please God when we tell the truth—we bring delight to Him. Can you imagine? You and I can bring delight to God—and it's so simple!

Today's true story from the Bible is about a man named Ananias and his wife Sapphira. Through what happened as a result of their lies, we will gain understanding of how God views truth.

USE AN OBJECT

Print the pictures from the Ministry Resource download and place them on the board (with tape or magnets) or in a pocket chart. As you teach the story, select a student to get the picture from the board when they hear it mentioned in the lesson. Once a student retrieves the picture, allow him to stand at the front of the class while you finish teaching. The following are words that have corresponding pictures:

Heart
Money
Land
Fear
Three Hours
Men

The Story

1. Church Members Give (Acts 4:32–37)

The Christians in the first church at Jerusalem, shortly after Jesus had ascended back to Heaven, were so excited about knowing the Lord. They shared the gospel and were thrilled when someone new trusted Jesus as their Saviour. They truly loved each person in the church—it was their new family.

Galatians 3:26

26   For ye are all the children of God by faith in Christ Jesus.

But many of the members of that early church had come to Jerusalem from long distances to hear the gospel, and after they trusted Jesus as their Saviour, stayed in Jerusalem to be part of the church. These people were without jobs or homes and needed financial help.

So, as they saw the needs of those who suffered financial loss, the other Christians didn't say, "Oh, that's too bad. John needs a place to live. I hope he's okay. I hope someone helps him. I need to look out for myself."

Flash Card 9.1

Instead, these Christians rallied together to help each other. They didn't even think of the things they possessed as belonging to themselves. They knew their possessions belonged to God, and they decided to use them the way God would use them.

Psalm 24:1

1   The earth is the LORD'S, and the fulness thereof; the world, and they that dwell therein.

USE AN OBJECT

Allow a student to retrieve the land picture from the board and hold it in front of the class.

Many of those who had land decided to sell it and give the money to the apostles (the church leaders) so they could help those in need. The Bible mentions one man in particular—Barnabas—who sold land and brought the money to the apostles.

As the Christians gave from hearts of love and trust in the Lord, everyone's needs were met. As the church grew in number, the Christians grew in the Lord, with hearts full of joy and peace and trust in the Lord.

But even in this joyous time when so many Christians' hearts were overflowing with the joy of giving and growing in the Lord, some people lacked faith that true joy comes from God. They tried to find joy for themselves. That's where the couple I mentioned earlier—Ananias and Sapphira—come into our story.

2. Ananias and Sapphira Make a Plan (Acts 5:2; 9a)

Flash Card 9.2

Ananias and his wife Sapphira saw the excitement when Barnabas brought the money for the land he had sold to the apostles. "Praise the Lord!" the Christians exclaimed. "Think of how God can use Barnabas' money to help the needy Christians!"

Ananias and Sapphira felt jealous of the praise Barnabas received. They wanted that kind of admiration. So they made a plan. Ananias may have said something like this:

"We have some land we can sell. We'll sell it and give some of the money to the apostles to distribute to the poor. But we won't give all the money—just most of it. We don't really need to say anything about keeping part of the money for ourselves. If the people want to think we gave it all, let them think it. But if we are actually asked if we gave all the money, we'll say we did. This will just be our little secret."

Sapphira agreed—she would lie about the money, if necessary.

USE AN OBJECT

Allow a student to retrieve the money picture from the board and hold it in front of the class.

3. Ananias Lies to the Holy Spirit (Acts 5:1–6)

Ananias and Sapphira went through with their plan. They sold the land and put part of the money away for themselves. Then Ananias brought the remaining money to the apostles.

But somehow God allowed the apostle Peter to know what really happened. "You didn't think I would know the truth, did you Ananias?" Peter asked. "Why have you allowed Satan to fill your heart with this lie?"

John 8:44

44 ...the devil...is a liar, and the father of it.

USE AN OBJECT

Allow a student to retrieve the heart picture from the board and hold it in front of the class.

"You haven't lied to men, but you have lied to the Holy Spirit of God! Wasn't the land your own, Ananias? You could have done whatever you wanted with it. You could have kept it, or you could have kept all the money after you sold it. You could have given part of the money to the church, or you could have given all the money to the church. It was your land—the choice was yours."

As Peter spoke these words, Ananias fell down and died. Some young men from the crowd got up, wrapped Ananias in a cloth, carried him out of the room, and buried him.

Everyone who was there was filled with fear.

USE AN OBJECT

Allow a student to retrieve the fear picture from the board and hold it in front of the class.

Flash Card 9.3

USE AN OBJECT

Allow a student to retrieve the picture of three fingers and hold it in front of the class.

USE AN OBJECT

Allow a student to retrieve the picture of the crowd of people and hold it in front of the class.

USE AN OBJECT

Using a black marker, draw a large heart on a poster board. Using Crayola Color Switchers markers, write the following words inside the heart with the invisible marker:

- Lying
- Deceitfulness
- Half truths
- Sin

Pointing to the heart on the poster board, tell the class that this heart is white and looks so clean and pure. Ask the students what kind of person they think this heart belongs to.

Then, take a red Crayola Color Switcher Marker and color the inside of the heart to reveal the hidden sins written previously.

Tell the class that only God can see our hearts.

4. Sapphira Lies (Acts 5:7–10)

About three hours later, Sapphira, not knowing what had happened to her husband, came to the apostles.

"Tell me, Sapphira," Peter questioned, "did you sell the land for so much?" (and he mentioned the amount Ananias had given.)

"Yes, that's the amount we sold it for," Sapphira lied.

"How is it that ye have agreed together to tempt [to try; to prove] the Spirit of the Lord?" Peter asked. "Your husband has died, and the same people who carried him to his burial have just now returned to carry you to your burial."

As Peter spoke these words, Sapphira fell down and died. And the young men who had carried out Ananias picked Sapphira up, carried her out, and buried her by her husband.

5. The Church Fears God (Acts 5:11)

Everyone who heard about the lies and deaths of Ananias and Sapphira was filled with fear. The church people said, "Wow! God is really God. He's serious about protecting His church, and He is serious about the consequences of lying! I'm going to believe and obey His Word."

And even the people who weren't Christians realized that the church was important to God and that God was to be feared.

APPLYING THE STORY

The Christians in the early church who gave financially to help their needy brothers and sisters in Christ believed that God was Who He says He is. They believed He always tells the truth. When God said He would meet the needs of those who give to the poor, they believed Him.

Proverbs 19:17

17 He that hath pity upon the poor lendeth unto the LORD; and that which he hath given will he pay him again.

So, they gave to the needy because they trusted God. And when they gave to the needy, God blessed them. God always blesses giving—sometimes with blessings we can see and touch—and sometimes with peace and joy in our hearts.

Not only do giving and sharing bring joy to the giver, but God instructs all Christians to give to those in need; and when we obey God, He blesses us.

Luke 6:38

38 Give, and it shall be given unto you; good measure, pressed down, and shaken together, and running over, shall men give into your bosom. For with the same measure that ye mete withal it shall be measured to you again.

Ananias and Sapphira decided to lie because they didn't trust God. They weren't living by the same grace that had saved them.

Ephesians 2:8

8 For by grace are ye saved through faith; and that not of yourselves: it is the gift of God:

To get saved, they had to trust in Jesus' death and resurrection as payment for their sin. That salvation was God's grace to them and to everyone who trusts Jesus as their Saviour, through faith, or trust.

So, they trusted Jesus to save them—they trusted God to be Who He said He was—the loving God Who sent His Son to be the payment for their sins.

But, when it came to living life after salvation, they weren't so sure they could trust God and His grace. They didn't really believe He was Who He says He is. They didn't believe He would bless trust and obedience; and they didn't believe sin really has consequences.

When they saw the needy Christians, they didn't trust God to bless their lives if they gave; so they didn't see God's blessings. They didn't prove God's truth through accepting His grace to give to those in need.

So, they lived their lives without seeing the wonderful works of grace God does through faith. They didn't trust God enough to believe He would bless truth.

1 Samuel 12:24

24 Only fear the LORD, and serve him in truth with all your heart: for consider how great things he hath done for you.

That's the way it is with lies. We tell them because we don't really believe that God is Who He says He is—One Who blesses truth. When we don't believe Him, we don't see Him do extra-special, exciting things in our lives; and we decide to live life from our own hearts, instead of from the truth of His Word.

> **TEACHER'S NOTE**
>
> **grace**—a free gift, unearned, undeserved, and unmerited. Grace is good things God gives us that we don't deserve.
>
> It's likely Ananias and Sapphira were saved, since they were part of the church the Bible calls "the multitude of them that believed" (Acts 4:32).

Jeremiah 17:9

9   The heart is deceitful above all things, and desperately wicked: who can know it?

We may not really believe there are consequences for lying. Maybe we have told lies in the past, and they kept us out of trouble. It becomes easy to lie. But there are always consequences for disobedience to God—lying included.

Numbers 32:23b

23   ...be sure your sin will find you out.

If we think telling a "white lie" or even a "big lie" will help us get what we want, we do it. We may believe a lie will make people think more highly of us. We may believe a lie will make us more popular. We may believe a lie will help us get an item we desire. We may just feel it would be more convenient in a particular situation to lie. We may believe a lie will keep us from getting in trouble.

But, when we tell these lies, we miss so much! We miss the closeness of a relationship with God based on truth. We miss living in freedom that comes through truth. We miss the blessings that come through truth.

John 8:32

32   And ye shall know the truth, and the truth shall make you free.

And we miss the joy of knowing we have brought delight to God!

Not only do we miss good things when we lie, but we, like Ananias and Sapphira, have to experience the consequences of lying.

- Our words won't be important words that will last and help others.

Proverbs 12:19

19   The lip of truth shall be established for ever: but a lying tongue is but for a moment.

- Our words will hurt others.

Proverbs 26:28

28   A lying tongue hateth those that are afflicted by it; and a flattering mouth worketh ruin.

TEACHER'S NOTE

You may wish to add more examples of blessings through speaking the truth and/or consequences of lying.

Perhaps you could include a personal testimony of a blessing resulting from truth telling or a sad consequence of lying in your own life.

Personal illustrations such as these allow your students to connect with you.

- Lying creates distance between us and the Lord.

Psalm 101:7

7   He that worketh deceit shall not dwell within my house: he that telleth lies shall not tarry in my sight.

- Parents and others won't trust us.

Proverbs 20:11

11   Even a child is known by his doings, whether his work be pure, and whether it be right.

Can you think of some ways we may lie that might not seem like an actual lie? (Allow response.)

- Saying we saw something we didn't or didn't see something we did
- Saying we did something we didn't or didn't do something we did
- Saying someone else did something they didn't do
- Cheating on a test
- Not telling the whole story to hide facts
- Giving a false impression
- Even lying to ourselves

Psalm 51:6

6   Behold, thou desirest truth in the inward parts: and in the hidden part thou shalt make me to know wisdom.

Remember, the reason we choose to tell any form of lie is that we don't really believe God. We don't believe that He will bless truth and punish lies.

Ananias and Sapphira's mistake was that they proudly trusted in themselves, rather than in God's grace. They didn't look beyond what they thought and understood to the truth of God's grace.

Isaiah 55:8

8   For my thoughts are not your thoughts, neither are your ways my ways, saith the LORD.

James 4:6

6   But he giveth more grace. Wherefore he saith, God resisteth the proud, but giveth grace unto the humble.

Ananias and Sapphira didn't believe God would bless their lives if they just trusted Him, and so they lied. Ananias and Sapphira missed so much:

- They missed a close walk with God.

- They missed knowing God's delight when a person tells the truth.

- They missed seeing God do great things in their lives.

Where are you in this area? Do you know the joy of bringing delight to God by regularly telling the truth? Do you believe God is Who He says He is, and trust Him with your heart and with your words?

Speaking lies is such a sad thing in a Christian's life. When a Christian is untruthful, it is because they are not believing the truthfulness of God; but God is always truthful. Man lies, but God never does.

Numbers 23:19

19 God is not a man, that he should lie; neither the son of man, that he should repent: hath he said, and shall he not do it? or hath he spoken, and shall he not make it good?

Every word God has ever spoken is true. Every promise He has ever made He has kept, and He will always do so.

Believe God's promises, accept His grace to trust Him, and bring delight to Him.

If you are struggling with lying (and almost everyone does at some time in their lives), tell God about your struggle. Right now, ask Him to forgive you. Accept the grace He gives you to tell the truth when you are tempted to lie. Every time you are tempted, believe that God's way is better.

Ephesians 4:25

25 Wherefore putting away lying, speak every man truth with his neighbour: for we are members one of another.

TEACHER'S NOTE

You may wish to offer to find some Bible promises that relate to individual student's struggles with lying due to not trusting God in a particular area.

If they privately share a struggle with you, offer to bring verses relating to their struggle the following week.

REVIEW GAME/QUESTIONS

Materials Needed

True/False cards from Ministry Resource download

Clothespins (one for each student)

Set Up

Print and cut two sets of True/False cards from Ministry Resource download

Arrange the class into two teams that can easily pass the cards in relay style from back to front.

Give each student a clothespin and assign helpers to assist each team.

Playing the Game

Divide the class into two teams and arrange the teams to sit in a straight line from the front of the class to the back of the class.

Give the last student in each row one True card and one False card.

Ask a True or False question from the list below, and allow the student to select the card he thinks is right. The student will place the card on his clothespin and pass it to the student in front of him who will retrieve it with his own clothespin. This relay continues until the card reaches the student in the first seat. The card can only be passed with a clothespin. If hands are used, the team forfeits that round.

The first team to select the correct card and pass it to the front (using only clothespins) wins that round.

Next, instruct the students to rotate seats, with the student sitting in front moving to the back and everyone shifting forward. Continue asking questions and passing the cards until everyone has had a turn to select a True or False card (or until there are no more questions). If additional questions are needed, you can borrow questions from previous lessons for further review.

The team to win the most rounds wins the game.

1. There really is such a thing as a "little white lie."
   Answer: False, all lies are sin.

2. Telling the truth brings delight to God.
   Answer: True

3. Some of the Christians in the early church kept their homes and were given jobs by the religious leaders.
   Answer: False, the Christians were persecuted by religious leaders.

4. The early Christians believed their possessions belonged to God.
    Answer: True

5. Ananias and Sapphira lied about the money because they wanted people to think they were good Christians.
    Answer: True

6. Peter said that Ananias had lied to the church.
    Answer: False, Peter said that Ananias had lied to the Holy Spirit.

7. Ananias and Sapphira both fell down and died.
    Answer: True

8. Ananias and Sapphira trusted in God and His Word
    Answer: False, they trusted in themselves.

9. We can miss blessings when we lie rather than trust God.
    Answer: True

10. God can lie.
    Answer: False, God can never lie.

Teaching the Memory Verse

Proverbs 12:22

22 Lying lips are abomination to the LORD: but they that deal truly are his delight.

Materials Needed

Memory Verse Flashcards from the Ministry Resource download

Lemon wedges (one per student)

Tootsie Pop (one per student)

Teaching the Verse

Lying is an abomination. It tastes bitter to the Lord. But, when we tell the truth, it is His delight!

Proceed to read a list of statements to your class. Some statements should be true and some should be false. Statements can be simple, such as:

- The sky is green.

- The grass is blue.

- The sun is hot.

If a statement is false, the students can lick the lemon wedge. If the statement is true, they can lick the Tootsie Pop.

After the statements have been read, the students may hold their lollipops and lemon wedges as they read the verse together several times from the Memory Verse Flashcards. When they say the phrase, "Lying lips are abomination to the LORD," they can hold up the lemon wedge. When they recite the phrase, "but they that deal truly are his delight," they can hold up the Tootsie Pop.

OBJECT LESSON—Covering Lies

Materials Needed

Glass jar filled halfway with water

A quarter

Pennies—one per student

Lesson

Place the quarter at the bottom of the glass jar of water.

Tell the students that the quarter represents one lie. (You can give an example of a lie for sake of the illustration.)

Distribute one penny to each student, and let the class know that each penny represents an attempt to cover up the original lie. (You can provide examples of excuses or lies given to cover up the lie.)

Instruct each student to walk by the jar and drop their penny into the jar, trying to cover the lie. When all of the students have participated, it is very likely that the entire quarter will be covered.

Application

Telling the truth is much easier than remembering all the things we have said to cover up the lie. Look at how many little excuses and lies we had to drop into the jar, just to cover up the original lie! (If the students were not able to cover the quarter, say something similar to, "Look at how many other lies it still would have taken to cover this one lie!")

Encourage your students to tell the truth and remind them that it is always easier to trust God and speak the truth than it is to keep track of all the lies you've spoken.

CRAFT—What Is Hiding in Your Heart?

Supplies

Ananias & Sapphira Puzzle printable from the Ministry Resource download

Children's scissors (one per student, if possible)

Crayons (If you choose the black and white puzzle printable)

Heart-shaped box or container (one per student)

Instructions

1. Print the puzzle printable on to cardstock and give one per student. (If you print off the puzzle in black and white, allow ample time for the children to color.)
2. Give each student a pair of children's scissors. Instruct each student to cut his or her puzzle in pieces. (The teacher and class assistants should show the students how to cut out the puzzle, allowing them to use their imagination for the size and shapes.)
3. Put the puzzle pieces into a heart box or container.

Application

Ananias and Sapphira hid sin and lies in their heart. Instead, God wants us to hide His Word in our heart to keep us from sinning! This week, assemble your puzzle and review our memory verse. Hide it in your heart, so you will not sin against God.

ADDITIONAL RESOURCES

Find the following items on the Ministry Resource download:

- Coloring Page (for younger children)
- Activity Page (for older children)
- Student Take-Home Paper
- PowerPoint Presentation

Suggested Classroom Schedule

Before Class	Complete attendance record. Provide students with coloring pages/activity pages.
Opening	Welcome
Prayer	Prayer requests and praise reports from the children
Song Time	
Memory Verse	Romans 15:1
Song Time	
Object Lesson	Greetings of Encouragement
Bible Lesson	Barnabas
Application/Invitation	Help saved students apply lesson. Invite unsaved students to receive Christ.
Snack	KIND Bars
Review Game/ Questions	
Craft	Encouraging Notecards
Closing	Give announcements and pray. Distribute take-home papers.

Lesson Ten Overview

Barnabas
Theme—Encouragement

Scripture
Acts 4:32–37

Memory Verse
Romans 15:1— *"We then that are strong ought to bear the infirmities of the weak, and not to please ourselves."*

Lesson Outline
Introducing the Story

Joses grew up just an ordinary boy, doing ordinary things. But somewhere along the line, he decided to give himself to the Lord to be an encourager. Eventually, the apostles gave Joses the nickname *Barnabas*, which meant "son of encouragement."

Telling the Story

1. **Barnabas Encourages Through His Money**
   (Acts 4:32–37)—Flashcard 10.1

2. **Barnabas Encourages Through His Influence**
   (Acts 9:26–27)—Flashcard 10.2

3. **Barnabas Encourages Through His Words**
   (Acts 11:19–26)

4. **Barnabas Encourages by Going** *(Acts 13:1–3)*
   —Flashcard 10.3

Applying the Story

Barnabas could encourage the people God intended for him to encourage because Barnabas went where God sent him. God can lead you, as well, to minister to another's heart in just the way He knows they need. Be a Barnabas for someone else, and if you feel the need for encouragement, don't be afraid to ask God to send a Barnabas your way.

LESSON TEN
10 Barnabas
Theme: Encouragement

TEACHER'S CHECKLIST

- ❏ Read Acts 4:32–37; Acts 9:26–27; Acts 11:19–26; Acts 13:1–3.
- ❏ Study Lesson Ten.
- ❏ Flash cards 10.1–10.3.
- ❏ Prepare snack—KIND Bars.
- ❏ Gather for review game—10 3x5 cards and 1 pen for each student.
- ❏ Gather for teaching the memory verse— Memory Verse Flashcards from the Ministry Resource download, 5 styrofoam cups, several books.
- ❏ Gather for object lesson—greeting cards.
- ❏ Gather for craft—card stock, stickers, scraps of paper, scissors, glue sticks.
- ❏ Print Memory Verse Flashcards from the Ministry Resource download.
- ❏ Print and duplicate Coloring Pages or Activity Pages on the Ministry Resource download (one per student).
- ❏ Print and duplicate Take-Home Paper on the Ministry Resource download (one per student).

SCRIPTURES

Acts 4:32–37

32 And the multitude of them that believed were of one heart and of one soul: neither said any of them that ought of the things which he possessed was his own; but they had all things common.

33 And with great power gave the apostles witness of the resurrection of the Lord Jesus: and great grace was upon them all.

34 Neither was there any among them that lacked: for as many as were possessors of lands or houses sold them, and brought the prices of the things that were sold,

35 And laid them down at the apostles' feet: and distribution was made unto every man according as he had need.

MEMORY VERSE

Romans 15:1
"We then that are strong ought to bear the infirmities of the weak, and not to please ourselves."

36   And Joses, who by the apostles was surnamed Barnabas, (which is, being interpreted, The son of consolation,) a Levite, and of the country of Cyprus,

37   Having land, sold it, and brought the money, and laid it at the apostles' feet.

BIBLE LESSON

Introducing the Story

TEACHER'S NOTE

infirmity —weakness; feebleness; failing (of body, mind, resolution, etc.)

Did you know that people didn't used to have last names? Think back to Bible days. We know of Adam, Eve, Abraham, Sarah, Joseph, Moses, Ruth, David, John, Mary, and many others. But we know them only by their first names.

As people began to be given last names (also called surnames), whether to distinguish people with the same first names from each other for convenience, or for business purposes, or for whatever reason, the names were often taken from traits about the person.

Sometimes the names came from traits having to do with relationships. A son of John might have been given the surname Johnson.

TEACHER'S TIP

You may wish to research meanings of your student's last names prior to this lesson. You can then share those meanings.

Use their name meanings to encourage them for specific character traits you see in them related to their name meanings. If a name meaning doesn't seem to lend itself to a positive characteristic, encourage that student in another area.

Other surnames were given because of a person's occupation. A man who was a fisherman might have been given the surname Fisher. A wood worker might have been given the surname Carpenter.

Other surnames came from a person's physical characteristics. A person who wasn't very tall might have been given the surname Short. A tall person might have been given the surname Long.

Surnames were also derived from a person's personality, habits, or character traits. Someone with a cheery personality who was known to whistle often may have been surnamed Whistler. A person who was known to have a lot of emotional ups and downs might have been given the surname Moody. A muscular person might have been given the surname Strong.

Does anyone here know the meaning of your last name? (Allow students to respond.)

In a way, many surnames began as a type of nickname. Just like nicknames, they were usually given to a person by others, rather than a person taking them on themselves:

- There's Steve the Fisher (later became Steve Fisher)

- Have you seen Bill, John's son? (later became Bill Johnson)

- Do you know Matthew the Whistler? (later became Matthew Whistler)

All of us here have surnames (last names) because surnames have been adapted into our culture (way of life). But not everyone has a nickname. Have you ever wished for a nickname?

Many people would like a nickname that relates to something they are proud of, something they would like to be known for. Sometimes a person will desire a particular nickname and will ask other people to start calling them by that name; but those types of nicknames rarely stick. Nicknames usually come from what others notice about us—whether good or bad.

If you could have any nickname in the world, what would you choose? (Allow students to respond, being careful to direct for appropriate responses.)

Here's an interesting question: If the Lord were going to give nicknames, what types of nicknames do you think He would like to be able to give? (Allow for response.) He would like to give nicknames based on our close walk with Him and what we allow Him to do in our lives. He would like to give nicknames based on our love, kindness, generosity, mercy, patience, faithfulness.

Those names would be names like Jason the Kind, Sarah the Merciful, Kristen the Faithful. Those are the kind of nicknames I would like to be given.

The man in today's true story from the Bible was given a nickname by his friends, and it became his surname.

> **TEACHER'S TIP**
>
> If you had a nickname in the past, especially one that caused you pain or embarrassment, many students would connect with your sharing it and the story behind it.
>
> Likely one or more of your students have been given unkind nicknames, and hearing your similar account would be an affirmation that says, "I understand—I've been there."

The Story

1. Barnabas Encourages through His Money (Acts 4:32–37)

When he was born, his parents named him Joses, (pronounced jo'sez) a common, ordinary name of his day. There were many Joseses (which is the same name as Joseph). Joses grew up just an ordinary boy, doing ordinary things.

But somewhere along the line, Joses made a decision to not be just ordinary. "I'm going to give my life to something bigger than myself. I'm going to help other people. I'm going to encourage them when they're down. I'm going to give what I have to help meet their needs. I'm going to be there for them. I'm going to help others be successful in their walk with the Lord."

And he did. Joses gave himself to the Lord to be an encourager—one who lifts others.

Sometime in his life, Joses trusted Jesus as his Saviour from sin, (See Acts 4:32—"the multitude of them that believed") and he became part of the first church at Jerusalem, shortly after Jesus ascended up to Heaven.

> **DRAW IT!**
>
> HELLO MY NAME IS
>
> # JOSES

> **DRAW IT!**
>
>

Flash Card 10.1

The leaders of the first church were the apostles—the men who had been Jesus' disciples when He lived on this earth. The apostles couldn't help but notice Joses. He was always helping people. "Can I lend you a hand?" he would offer to whoever was working on a task. He helped the needy church members. He encouraged the hurting. He was always there, doing whatever he could.

"There goes Joses the encourager," they would say to each other. "He is an example to us all—he gives his time, he gives his money, he gives kind words—he is always lifting others."

And so, the apostles gave Joses the nickname Barnabas, which, in the Greek language they spoke, meant "son of encouragement." It became his surname, and, finally, everyone just called him Barnabas.

We heard of Barnabas in our lesson last week. Although many people sold their land to help the financially needy church members, Barnabas was the only one mentioned by name. "My money is the Lord's," Barnabas believed deep in his heart, "and I will use it the way He would use it."

DRAW IT!

SOLD

Philippians 2:3–4

3 Let nothing be done through strife or vainglory; but in lowliness of mind let each esteem other better than themselves.

4 Look not every man on his own things, but every man also on the things of others.

DRAW IT!

Barnabas used his money to encourage others.

2. Barnabas Encourages through His Influence (Acts 9:26–27)

The Jewish religious leaders persecuted the Christians for their belief in salvation through Jesus Christ. One of the most known for persecuting Christians was a man named Saul. His main desire in life was to see Christians thrown into prison and killed for their faith in Jesus. All the Christians were afraid of Saul.

But Saul trusted Jesus as his Saviour, and he became a different person.

2 Corinthians 5:17

17 Therefore if any man be in Christ, he is a new creature: old things are passed away; behold, all things are become new.

God had a wonderful plan for the rest of Saul's life—He was going to use him to lead many people to salvation in Jesus Christ. In fact, God was going to use Saul one day to write much of the New Testament!

Saul went to Jerusalem to join with the apostles to preach the Word of God.

"I want you to know, I am a new man," Saul said to the apostles. "In the past I persecuted Christians, but now I have trusted Christ, and I want to serve Him."

The apostles knew the terrible things Saul had done to Christians. They saw him hold the coats of those who had stoned the godly man Stephen to death, simply because he preached the truth about Jesus. They saw Saul go from house to house having their own church members arrested and thrown into prison.

Many Christians had left Jerusalem to escape persecution, and many were imprisoned by Saul. The apostles knew Saul was a leader in this terrible persecution, and they didn't trust him.

"We know who you are and what you've done," the apostles said. "You are not a follower of Christ."

But Barnabas, the encourager, listened to Saul. "What has happened in your life, Saul?" he asked. And Saul told him how he had trusted in Jesus and that God had already used him to preach in Damascus, a city outside of Israel.

"I believe you, Saul; and I believe God has already used you, and that He is going to use you greatly." Barnabas greatly encouraged Saul.

"Come with me, Saul. I have worked with the apostles, and they trust me. We're going to talk to the apostles together!" And Barnabas brought Saul to the apostles and told them about Saul's amazing salvation and that God had already used him to preach boldly at Damascus about Jesus Christ.

The apostles believed Barnabas, and they allowed Saul to join with them. The apostles saw God greatly use Saul as a preacher and teacher.

Barnabas used his influence to encourage Saul.

3. Barnabas Encourages through His Words (Acts 11:19–26)

The Christians who had fled for their lives began preaching the gospel wherever they went, and many people trusted Christ. One such place was the city of Antioch.

"Hey, have you heard what's happened in Antioch?" someone brought news to the apostles. "Some of the Christians who had to flee Jerusalem have gone to Antioch and preached the gospel to the Greeks there; and a great number of them have believed on Jesus!"

DRAW IT!

PREACH

Flash Card 10.2

DRAW IT!

GOOD JOB!

"We need to send someone to see what's happening there," the disciples said. "And who would be a greater encourager for them than Barnabas? He's a good man, and he is filled with the Holy Spirit. We know God will use him."

When Barnabas saw all the Christians in Antioch, he was filled with joy. "God is doing wonderful things here," Barnabas encouraged the Antioch Christians. "I see His grace in your lives; and that same grace that brought you salvation will help you walk with the Lord. Purpose in your hearts to walk closely with Him. Follow Him wherever He leads. Obey each direction He gives along the way. Talk to God, and ask Him for guidance. He will continue working in you and through you."

Barnabas trusted the Lord to work through him and through all the Christians, and that is what the Lord did. As Barnabas encouraged the people, the Holy Spirit convicted hearts of their need for salvation, and many more were saved.

"We need help," Barnabas realized. "There are so many Christians, and so many more people to become Christians that we need someone else to lead and encourage them." Barnabas found Saul and brought him to Antioch.

Saul and Barnabas stayed in Antioch for a year, preaching the gospel and teaching the Christians how to grow in the Lord. Under the leadership of Saul and Barnabas, the church at Antioch became strong—the first place the disciples were given the name Christians.

DRAW IT!

Flash Card 10.3

4. Barnabas Encourages by Going (Acts 13:1–3)

The Antioch church leaders walked closely with the Lord. They prayed constantly, asking God to direct them.

The Holy Spirit spoke to their hearts, "I have a work for Saul and Barnabas." And Barnabas and Saul became the first missionaries.

Barnabas went with Saul (now called Paul) from city to city, preaching the gospel and then discipling the new believers (teaching them how to grow in the Lord). They started many churches, and as they traveled, they returned to churches they had already started, encouraging them in their walk with the Lord.

Paul has become known as one of the greatest Christian leaders of all time, and Barnabas has become known as one of the greatest encouragers of all time—the one who lifted Paul and encouraged him to become what God wanted him to be.

APPLYING THE STORY

God used Barnabas the encourager to greatly impact the early church. The church needed an encourager, and encouragement was the way of life Barnabas had chosen—not to become great or well-known, but to serve the Lord.

Barnabas didn't plan to become the encourager of one of the greatest Christians who ever lived—he just planned to encourage everyone he met:

- **He encouraged through giving.**

  Barnabas gave a great sum of money to help needy Christians—all the money he received from selling a piece of property. But before Barnabas gave a large amount of money, he gave smaller things. He believed everything he owned—great or small—belonged to the Lord.

  We don't all have property to sell, but we do all have something. God knows exactly what you have, and He would never ask you to give anything He hasn't already given you. Ask the Lord, "What do I have? What can I give?"

  What God directs you to give may seem so small and insignificant to you, but if God has given it to you, He can use it. Trust Him, and give what He leads you to give.

- **He encouraged through his influence (the fact that the apostles trusted him).** When the apostles didn't trust Saul because they knew what he had been and what he had done to Christians, Barnabas sought Saul out, to listen to him and to help him. After he heard Saul's story, Barnabas used his influence to encourage the apostles to trust and accept Saul.

  We don't all have great influence with Christian leaders, but we do all have some influence. Ask the Lord, "How can I use my influence to help someone who is being rejected?"

  Is there a person at school or church who is usually alone? Could you encourage others to include them in your activities? Or, if you are alone, could you just invite them to do something with you?

  Think of when you have felt rejected. Did someone believe in you and reach out to you? If they did, think of how God could use you to life up someone who is rejected. If no one reached out to you, think of what it would have meant to you if someone had reached out to you. You can be the encourager.

- **He encouraged through his words.** When he was sent to Antioch to see the new church, he was overjoyed at what God was doing in the lives of the new believers. He began doing what he did best—encouraging the Christians. He spoke words of encouragement about their salvation. He spoke words to encourage them to keep walking with the Lord. He spoke words to encourage them to grow in the Lord.

  Barnabas wanted the Christians of Antioch to grow so much that he found Saul to help them.

  We don't all have a huge church full of new believers to encourage, but we do all have this church. And in this very church, God wants us to encourage others.

Hebrews 10:25

25 Not forsaking the assembling of ourselves together, as the manner of some is; but exhorting one another: and so much the more, as ye see the day approaching.

Ask the Lord, "How can I encourage people at church? Who should I start with?"

If you share with a friend something the Lord taught you in your Bible reading, your friend will be encouraged to read his Bible.

If you share with someone an answer God gave to your prayer, that person will be encouraged to spend more time talking to the Lord in prayer.

If you mention to a person that you notice something the Lord is doing in their life, they will be encouraged to thank the Lord and to ask Him to work even more in their life.

If you share with someone that you saw them do something kind and loving for someone, they will be encouraged to do more kind and loving things.

Your words can be the greatest encouragement to someone. Think of when God has lifted your heart through something someone said to you. They may not even have realized how much what they said encouraged you.

Encouraging words don't have to only be spoken; they can be written. Sometimes a note of encouragement is exactly what a person needs to lift their spirit.

- **He encouraged through going.** When God wanted to send the first missionaries ever out to share the gospel, He chose Barnabas, the encourager. And Barnabas went where God sent him.

  God is not likely sending you to a far away land to share the gospel at this point in your life, but He does send you places where you can share the gospel. Do you go to school? You can share the gospel with other students. Do you go to the park? To the store? Where does He send you? God will use you to share the gospel wherever He directs you in your life, right now.

  Barnabas could encourage the people God intended for him to encourage because Barnabas went where God sent him.

We never know what others are going through in their hearts and in their lives. But God knows everything. He can lead your heart to minister to another's heart in just the way He knows they need, with just what He has given you.

And if you, yourself, are in great need of encouragement, be a Barnabas for someone else; and don't be afraid to ask God to send a Barnabas your way.

REVIEW GAME/QUESTIONS

Materials Needed

10 3x5 cards for each student
1 pen for each student

Set Up

Place 2–5 chairs at the front of the class (adapt based on the number of children in your class).
Label each chair with point values (20 points, 40 points, 80 points, 100 points, etc).

Playing the Game

Divide the class into two teams. Ask a question to the entire class. The students can write the answer down on their paper and race to sit the chairs in the front of the class.

Once the chairs are filled with students, double check their answers for accuracy and total the points earned for each team. (All students can race to the chairs, so one team could potentially receive all the points. Alternatively, a student from Team One who sits in a chair with high point value, could still contribute to his team even if students from Team Two fill the other chairs of lower point values.)

Ask a class worker to keep a tally of the points. The team with the most points at the end of the game wins.

Variation: If your students are too young to write their answers on paper, arrange only two chairs in the front. Assign a class worker to write down the team answer on a piece of paper and to pick a student to race to the chairs.

1. What was Barnabas' first name?

   Answer: Joses

2. What did Barnabas do when some church members needed financial help?

   Answer: He sold his property, and gave the money to the church to help the struggling people.

3. Why did the apostles give Joses the nickname Barnabas? What does Barnabas mean?

   Answer: Barnabas means "son of encouragement." They nicknamed him Barnabas because he consistently encouraged others.

4. Who was the apostle that Barnabas greatly encouraged through his influence?

   Answer: Saul, or Paul

5. What did Barnabas do to encourage Saul when the disciples were afraid of him?

   Answer: He told the disciples that Saul was saved and that he was a changed man.

6. Why did the apostles send Barnabas to the church at Antioch?

   Answer: The people there needed encouragement, and the disciples knew Barnabas would encourage them.

7. Who became the very first missionaries?

   Answer: Barnabas and Saul

8. Where was the first place the disciples were called "Christians"?

   Answer: Antioch

9. What are some ways we can be encouragers in other people's lives?

   Answer: Answers will vary, but will likely include examples under the headings giving, influence, words, and going.

10. Where are some of the places God sends you where you can share the gospel with others?

Answer: Answers will vary.

Teaching the Memory Verse

Romans 15:1

1   We then that are strong ought to bear the infirmities of the weak, and not to please ourselves.

Materials Needed

Memory Verse Flashcards from the Ministry Resource download

5 styrofoam cups

Several books (preferably hardback)

Teaching the Verse

Our verse today tells us to bear the infirmities of the weak. God wants us to be like Barnabas—to bear the burdens of others. On a table or on the floor at the front of the class, place one Styrofoam cup, face down.

Stack one book on the cup, and recite the verse as a class. Call on a student to place another book on the cup, and again, instruct the entire verse to say the class. Continue stacking books and reciting the verse until the cup collapses under the weight of the books.

Variation: Cover hardback books with brown paper, and write one word from the verse on the spine of each book. As the students place the books on the cup, they can do so in order, finding the correct word from the stack of books placed to the side of the cup.

OBJECT LESSON —Greetings of Encouragement

Materials Needed

A compilation of greeting cards (get well soon, thinking of you, thank you, etc.)

Lesson

Explain to the class that you have picked up several greeting cards with different messages on the front and inside. As you read each greeting card, ask the students of situations for which the greeting card would be appropriate. (ie; a "get well soon" card could be given to a sick relative, a "thank you" card could be given to a parent, teacher or pastor, etc.)

Application

If any card can be used as a source of encouragement for a member in your church, have the students sign their names and write a message of encouragement to those people. Encourage your class to look for ways to be an encouragement to others throughout this week.

CRAFT—Encouraging Notecards

Supplies

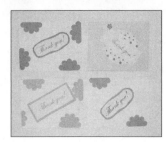

Card stock in an assortment of colors (Cut into 4.25 by 5 inches)
Stickers
Scraps of paper
Scissors
Glue sticks

Instructions

1. Give each student 5 sheets of cut card stock.
2. Give each student stickers, scraps of paper, scissors and a glue stick.
3. Instruct the students to make 5 cards and write an encouraging note to their pastor, parents, siblings, teacher, shut-in, or widow in the church.

Application

It doesn't take much to be an encouragement to others. Sometimes, even a simple note can be a blessing to another person. Look for ways this week to be an encourager!

ADDITIONAL RESOURCES

Find the following items on the Ministry Resource download:

- Coloring Page (for younger children)
- Activity Page (for older children)
- Student Take-Home Paper
- PowerPoint Presentation

Suggested Classroom Schedule

Before Class	Complete attendance record. Provide students with coloring pages/activity pages.
Opening	Welcome
Prayer	Prayer requests and praise reports from the children
Song Time	
Memory Verse	Hebrews 13:6
Song Time	
Object Lesson	Superhero Courage
Bible Lesson	Paul
Application/Invitation	Help saved students apply lesson. Invite unsaved students to receive Christ.
Snack	Lion Cupcakes
Review Game/ Questions	
Craft	Paul Mini Activity Book
Closing	Give announcements and pray. Distribute take-home papers.

Lesson Eleven Overview

Paul
Theme—Boldness

Scripture
Acts 9:1-6

Memory Verse
Hebrews 13:6— *"So that we may boldly say, The Lord is my helper, and I will not fear what man shall do unto me."*

Lesson Outline
Introducing the Story
Saul started out with an enormous amount of people agreeing with him, encouraging him to continue in his own "bold" acts. But, after he trusted Jesus as his Saviour, he spoke out against the crowd that had agreed with him, and allowed God to give him true boldness.

Telling the Story
1. **Saul's Early Life** *(Acts 9; 22:3-24; Philippians 3:4-6) —Flashcard 11.1*

2. **Saul's Salvation** *(Acts 9; 26:12-18) —Flashcard 11.2*

3. **Saul Gains True Boldness** *(various accounts in Acts 9, 13, 14, 16, 17, 19, 27) —Flashcard 11.3*

Applying the Story
Boldness from the Lord gives us the confidence that the results are not as important as trusting and following the Lord. We can trust Him in every situation. Because Paul boldly stood for the Lord Jesus, God was able to use him to write thirteen books of the New Testament. Imagine what God can do through you when you allow Him to be bold through you!

LESSON ELEVEN
Paul
Theme: Boldness

TEACHER'S CHECKLIST

☐   Read Acts 9.

☐   Study Lesson Eleven.

☐   Flash cards 11.1–11.3.

☐   Prepare snack—Lion Cupcakes.

☐   Gather for "Use an Object"—Birth certificate, backpack, handcuffs, letters, flashlight, walking stick, superhero cape, red wax lips.

☐   Gather for object lesson—super hero cape.

☐   Gather for review game—Lion Face printable from Ministry Resource download, brown yarn, hole punch.

☐   Gather for teaching the verse— Memory Verse Flashcards and Pringles can cover printable from Ministry Resource download, one empty Pringles chips can, candy.

☐   Print for review game—Lion Face printable from Ministry Resource download.

☐   Print for teaching the verse—Memory Verse Flashcards and Pringles can cover printable from Ministry Resource download.

☐   Print for craft—*Life of Paul* mini activity book printable from Ministry Resource download.

☐   Print and duplicate Coloring Pages or Activity Pages on the Ministry Resource download (one per student).

☐   Print and duplicate Take-Home Paper on the Ministry Resource download (one per student).

SCRIPTURES

Acts 9:1–6

1   And Saul, yet breathing out threatenings and slaughter against the disciples of the Lord, went unto the high priest,

MEMORY VERSE

Hebrews 13:6
"So that we may boldly say, The Lord is my helper, and I will not fear what man shall do unto me."

2 And desired of him letters to Damascus to the synagogues, that if he found any of this way, whether they were men or women, he might bring them bound unto Jerusalem.

3 And as he journeyed, he came near Damascus: and suddenly there shined round about him a light from heaven:

4 And he fell to the earth, and heard a voice saying unto him, Saul, Saul, why persecutest thou me?

5 And he said, Who art thou, Lord? And the Lord said, I am Jesus whom thou persecutest: it is hard for thee to kick against the pricks.

6 And he trembling and astonished said, Lord, what wilt thou have me to do? And the Lord said unto him, Arise, and go into the city, and it shall be told thee what thou must do.

BIBLE LESSON

Introducing the Story

What would you give as the definition of the word boldness? (Allow students to respond.) Boldness means "confidence; assurance; courage; the trait of being willing to undertake things that involve risk or danger; bravery."

For the Christian, there are two types of boldness:

- The boldness that comes from inside your own heart, and is often stronger when others agree with you.

- The boldness that God gives when you follow His will and trust in Him to help you and give you strength.

The boldness that comes from your own heart could be the kind of boldness that even a bully might have. He may have a few tough guys behind him, picking on someone smaller than him. He might look bold and strong, but his boldness would be gone if someone bigger and stronger than him decided to pick on him.

The boldness that comes from your own heart could also be the kind of boldness someone might have to speak disrespectfully to a teacher when their friends are cheering them on. They might look bold to be willing to face the teacher's disapproval, but when their friends are gone, their boldness will be gone too.

The boldness that comes from God is the kind of boldness God gives us to tell the truth, even when we are facing punishment. It's the kind of boldness

God gives us to share the gospel when we are afraid. It's the kind of boldness God gives us to stand alone in our choices, even when it seems everyone else is choosing to participate in an activity that we know displeases the Lord.

If you believe something that not everyone believes, but you have a whole crowd of people agreeing with you and standing behind you, would it take the from-your-own-heart kind of boldness to say what you believe, or would it take the from-God kind of boldness? (Allow students to respond.)

If everyone around you says they are happy living life on their own and that believing in God is foolish, would it take the from-your-own-heart kind of boldness to say what you believe, or would it take the from-God kind of boldness? (Allow students to respond.)

Today we're going to talk about a man in the Bible who was absolutely full of the from-your-own-heart kind of boldness. He was so full of his own boldness, that many people were afraid of him.

Saul started out with an enormous amount of people agreeing with him, encouraging him to continue in his own "bold" acts. But, after he trusted Jesus as his Saviour from sin, he spoke out against the crowd that had agreed with him, and allowed God to give him true boldness.

The Story

1. Saul's Early Life (Acts 9; 22:3–24; Philippians 3:4–6)

Saul had every reason to feel like he was right when it came to religion. He was a Jew, and all his ancestors were Jews. They believed in God. Saul's parents brought him up to strictly follow the Jewish law God had given to the Israelites many years earlier.

When Saul became old enough, his parents sent him to Jerusalem, to the best teacher they knew—a man named Gamaliel—to teach him the Jewish law. Saul was an excellent student, and he was very careful to obey God's commands.

Saul and the other Jews believed that one day a Messiah would come to save them from their sins. The problem was, they didn't know the Messiah had come. His name was Jesus Christ, who died on the cross to suffer the punishment for our sins, rose from the dead three days later, and, finally, ascended back to Heaven. All those who trust in Him have eternal life. Trusting in Jesus is the only way to have eternal life—the only way to Heaven.

The more Saul studied, the more he wanted to stand up for God. And the more he studied the law God gave the Israelites, the more he wanted to teach it

> **USE AN OBJECT**
>
> Birth Certificate—Saul was born into a religious home (Acts 23:6, Philippians 3:3). Ask a student to stand at the front of the class and hold a birth certificate.

> **USE AN OBJECT**
>
> Backpack—Saul was a student of Gamaliel (Acts 22:3). Ask a student to stand at the front of the class and hold a backpack.

and defend it. Finally, Saul decided to become a Pharisee—one of the religious leaders and teachers of the law. Not only did the Pharisees teach the law, but they required other people to obey the law, and they added some of their own rules to it. "If you want to go to heaven," the Pharisees said, "you must follow God's law."

Now, this was also a problem, because the Jews had added to the law God gave. Now they were requiring people to follow the laws they made up, insisting that following their laws was the way to gain favor with God—the way to go to Heaven.

There was another problem, too. The way to gain favor with God was not through following any set of laws; it was through trusting Jesus' death on the cross as the complete payment for your sin. No one ever followed the Jewish laws perfectly—everyone sinned (including you and me). That's why God sent His Son to die on the cross. He paid for our sin so we wouldn't have to.

When Saul was grown, he agreed with the Jewish teachers so strongly that he began to speak out against the followers of Jesus—the Christians. The Jewish leaders were proud of Saul for following their beliefs.

The more he spoke against the Christians, the angrier Saul became at them. He seemed awfully bold as he began arresting Christians and having them thrown into prison.

Finally, Saul began to hate Christianity so much that he became a leader in persecuting Christians. He had them bound, imprisoned, and sometimes killed. He was even a leader in the stoning of the godly man, Stephen, who was killed for preaching about Jesus.

Acts 22:4

4   And I persecuted this way unto the death, binding and delivering into prisons both men and women.

Saul became known everywhere for his boldness in persecuting Christians. The Jewish leaders were so proud of him.

2. Saul's Salvation (Acts 9; 26:12–18)

But God had a plan for Saul, the bold persecutor of Christians, and God knew the best way to get Saul's attention.

After the stoning of Stephen, Saul's anger toward Christians became greater than ever. "They are going against everything I believe," Saul thought. "We can't

---

USE AN OBJECT

Handcuffs—Saul arrested Christians. Ask a student to stand at the front of the class and hold toy handcuffs.

Flash Card 11.1 →

---

have this anymore. We have to get rid of these followers of Jesus Christ, even if it means death! I'll go to the highest religious leader in the land, if I have to!"

And that's what Saul did. He went straight to the high priest. "We must stop these followers of Jesus from spreading their beliefs," Saul said. "If you give me letters requiring that all believers of Jesus are to be bound and imprisoned, I will carry those letters to the synagogues (Jewish worship centers) in Damascus. We will tie up all the followers of Jesus, and I will bring them back to Jerusalem to go on trial.

The high priest agreed with Saul, and he gave Saul the letters he requested. Saul must have seemed very bold as he started on the one hundred thirty mile trip to Damascus to arrest the Christians. It's easy to be bold when you have many people agreeing with you.

As Saul got near to Damascus, a strange thing happened—a miracle. A light from heaven suddenly shone around him. As Saul fell to the ground, he heard a voice speaking to him, "Saul, Saul, why do you persecute me?"

Although Saul knew the voice came from the Lord, Saul didn't know Him. Remember, it was Saul's hatred for Jesus that had caused him to persecute Christians. "Who are you?" Saul said to the voice that came from the bright light.

"I am Jesus—the one you are persecuting," the Lord answered. "The more you fight against me, the harder your life will be."

All of a sudden Saul knew and believed: Jesus Christ truly was God the Son! Saul began to shake with fear. "I haven't only been persecuting the followers of Jesus," Saul thought. "I have been persecuting Jesus Christ, the Son of God!" And Saul trusted in Jesus.

"Lord, what should I do now?" Saul asked. His bold, proud heart was now humble.

"Go into the city, and you will receive instruction," the Lord answered.

Saul stood up, ready to obey the Lord. "I can't see a thing," Saul thought. His eyesight was gone—he was blind. The men who were with Saul took him by the hand, and led him to Damascus.

God was already working in the hearts of people in Damascus, getting them ready to help Saul. The Lord spoke to a man named Ananias, "Go to a certain house and meet a man named Saul of Tarsus. He will be expecting you."

"But Lord, I have heard of this man. He has persecuted the believers in Jerusalem, and now he has authority to bind the believers here in Damascus and take us away!"

USE AN OBJECT

Letters—Saul asked for letters giving him the authority to persecute Christians (Acts 9:2). Ask a student to stand at the front of the class and hold letters.

Flash Card 11.2

USE AN OBJECT

Flashlight—A light from Heaven shone on him, and Saul met Jesus on the road to Damascus. (Acts 9:3). Ask a student to stand at the front of the class to hold a flashlight.

USE AN OBJECT

Walking Stick—After Saul met Jesus, he was blind (Acts 9:8). Ask a student to stand at the front of the class to hold the walking stick.

Flash Card 11.3

"Trust Me, Ananias," God said. "I have a special plan for Saul. He is going to carry my name to many people—to the Jews, to rulers, and to the Gentiles who have never heard of me. He is going to suffer for my sake."

Ananias trusted the Lord and went to meet Saul. He put his hands on Saul's head and said, "Brother Saul, the Lord Jesus sent me to you. Receive your sight back and be filled with the Holy Spirit."

Saul's sight returned immediately, and he was baptized, as God told all believers to do.

3. Saul Gains True Boldness (various accounts in Acts 9, 13, 14, 16, 17, 19, 27)

Saul's heart was no longer full of pride and of his own boldness. Saul came to love the Lord Jesus with all his heart, and he wanted only to know the Lord, to follow Him, and to make Him known to others.

Philippians 3:10

10   That I may know him, and the power of his resurrection, and the fellowship of his sufferings, being made conformable unto his death;

Saul was willing to do whatever it took to share the gospel with people. He spent time alone with the Lord, learning the truth of the Scriptures and learning who Jesus really was. When he finally returned to Damascus, he boldly preached the gospel in the synagogue—to the same people who were going to assist him in persecuting the believers there!

Saul's boldness no longer came from his own heart. He lived in the power of the Holy Spirit, who gave him the boldness to share the truth with those who believed it and with those who didn't. Saul was so aware that his boldness had to come from the Lord, that he asked Christians to pray that God would give him boldness.

Ephesians 6:19

19   And for me, that utterance may be given unto me, that I may open my mouth boldly, to make known the mystery of the gospel,

Now Saul, who had been the great persecutor of Christians, faced persecution himself. The religious leaders in Damascus plotted to kill him for preaching the same gospel he had persecuted (Acts 9:23–24).

Saul was rescued from the religious leaders and went on to boldly serve the Lord, often in the face of much danger.

- He, along with Barnabas, became one of the first missionaries, and he was given the name Paul. (Acts 13:1–5; 9).

- He was beaten and thrown in prison for preaching the gospel through the boldness God gave him (Acts 16:16–34). Note: Paul was imprisoned many times, and he wrote many of the Epistles from prison.

- He was stoned for preaching the gospel through the boldness God gave him (Acts 14:19).

- He was shipwrecked as a prisoner who preached the gospel through the boldness God gave him (Acts 27).

- He was persecuted in many cities for preaching the gospel through the boldness God gave him (Acts 9:29, 19:23).

- He preached the gospel to educated people, even though many of them mocked him (Acts 17:15–34).

Persecution wasn't the only thing that required Paul's boldness. He became a leader of many churches, and he needed boldness from the Lord to serve those churches when it wasn't easy. He needed boldness from the Lord to share God's truth with Christians who were not following the Lord as the Bible taught. He needed boldness from the Lord to love when people didn't love him back. He needed boldness from the Lord to share the gospel, in prison or out of prison.

APPLYING THE STORY

Have you ever, like Paul, been that one person facing others and saying something is right or wrong when everyone else is against you? (Allow students to respond.)

We will have many times in life where we need boldness from the Lord.

- When others are sharing that they believe the world was created by evolution or by chance, we need God's boldness to say that we believe God created the world, as the Bible teaches (Genesis 1:1; John 1:3).

TEACHER'S TIP

In 2 Corinthians 11:23–33, Paul speaks of the dangers and trials God brought him through as Paul ministered the gospel of grace. Most of the bulleted points to the left are cross references to the points in 2 Corinthians. You may wish to read this passage for yourself and find many more examples.

TEACHER'S TIP

Share an example from your own life when the Lord gave you boldness to stand for Him. This may have been in a soulwinning situation (or even just the ability to be a soulwinner, if you are a naturally shy person), a work or extended family related circumstance, or any situation where you stood against popular opinion.

- When a friend or relative says they are going to Heaven because they are a good person, we need God's boldness to lovingly share that the Bible teaches everyone is a sinner and it is only through trusting the blood Jesus shed on the cross that we can have our sins forgiven. Jesus is the only way to Heaven (John 14:6).

- When our friends are planning to do something the Lord has convicted us is not right for us as Christians, we need God's boldness to stand up for what we believe and not go along with them (1 Corinthians 15:58).

- When people are making fun of or bullying someone, we need God's boldness to wisely defend them (Psalm 82:4).

- When we are tempted to lie, we need God's boldness to tell the truth, not fearing the results (Ephesians 4:25).

- When we are tempted to feel ashamed for people to know we are Christians, we need God's boldness to share our love for Him (Romans 1:16). Note: This could include being ashamed to pray for our meal at a restaurant, etc.

You may never have to be bold in the face of imprisonment or death, but standing up for the Lord will sometimes bring consequences you would wish to avoid. That happened a lot to Paul. But Paul never regretted that he chose to walk in God's boldness.

Paul didn't need a whole crowd of people standing with him to speak boldly or act boldly for the Lord. He only needed the Lord with him. Sometimes the crowd was on Paul's side, and sometimes the crowd was against him. It was the Lord who gave Paul all the strength he needed to follow the Lord in each situation.

Boldness from the Lord gives us the confidence that the results are not as important as trusting and following the Lord. We can trust Him in every situation.

Romans 8:31

31 What shall we then say to these things? If God be for us, who can be against us?

Because Paul boldly stood for the Lord Jesus, God was able to use him to write thirteen books of the New Testament. Imagine what God can do through you when you allow Him to be bold through you!

REVIEW GAME/QUESTIONS

Materials Needed

Lion Face printable from Ministry Resource download

Brown yarn (cut into pieces of various lengths)

Hole punch

Set Up

Print the Lion Face on 8x10 or 11x17 cardstock. With a hole punch, put holes around the lion's face. Insert the varying lengths of yarn pieces in the holes to create a mane.

Playing the Game

When a student answers a review question correctly, they can come to the front and pull out one piece of yarn. That student can remain up front until the second question is asked. The next student to answer correctly, comes to the front and pulls out a piece of yarn, as well. The student with the longer piece remains at the front and stays there until another student picks a longer piece of yarn. The student with the longest piece of yarn at the end of the game wins.

1. What are two different types of boldness a Christian can have?
   Answer: From-your-own-heart boldness, and the from-God kind of boldness

2. Who was Saul's religious teacher?
   Answer: Gamaliel

3. What was Saul taught was the way to go to Heaven?
   Answer: Obeying the Jewish law

4. Why is it a problem for the Jewish teachers to say that the people had to obey the law to get to Heaven?
   Answer: The only way to Heaven is through trusting Jesus as your Saviour from sin.

5. What were some of the ways Saul persecuted Christians?
   Answer: He had them bound, imprisoned, and sometimes even killed.

6. What strange thing happened to Saul as he was traveling to Damascus?
   Answer: A very bright light from Heaven shone around him, Jesus spoke to him, and he got saved.

7. What was Saul's name changed to?
    Answer: Paul

8. What were some things Paul did that required boldness from God?
    Answer: He became one of the first missionaries, was beaten, stoned, and thrown in prison for preaching the Gospel; was shipwrecked as a prisoner who preached the Gospel; was persecuted in many cities for preaching the Gospel; preached the Gospel to educated people even when they mocked him; he became a leader of many churches and served them when it wasn't easy; he shared God's truth with Christians who weren't following the Lord, and he loved when people didn't love him back.

9. What are some things that you might need boldness from the Lord for?
    Answer: Answers will vary. Standing up for what you believe is right, telling people the Gospel, telling the truth, defending someone who's being bullied, sharing our love for God.

10. What did Paul ask Christians to do so he would have boldness?
    Answer: Pray for him.

11. Who do we need to be with us when the crowd is against us?
    Answer: God

Teaching the Memory Verse

Hebrews 13:6

6   So that we may boldly say, The Lord is my helper, and I will not fear what man shall do unto me.

Materials Needed

Memory Verse Flashcards from the Ministry Resource download
One empty Pringles chips can
Pringles can cover printable from Ministry Resource download
Candy

Set Up

Prior to class, download the Pringles chips can cover printable and glue to the Pringles chips can.

Teaching the Verse

Have the students recite a few times as a class. Then, instruct the students to stand.

Once the students stand, hand the lion can to the first student. The lion can is passed from student to student around the room, each student saying the next word of the memory verse. When the lion can is passed to the last student who says, "me," that student can take a piece of candy out of the can and sit down. Continue playing until each student has received a piece of candy. (To keep the students who have been seated engaged, have the class say the verse together after a few people have received a piece of candy.)

OBJECT LESSON—Superhero Courage

Materials Needed

Super hero cape

Lesson

Call on a student to wear the super hero cape and ask the class a series of questions related to super hero power and courage. (What is your favorite super hero power? Who would you help if you had super hero power?)

Application

When it comes to following Jesus, we need power beyond ourselves. Like superheroes, we are given a special power from God. We may not be able to fly or possess super human strength. But, God does give us boldness to follow Jesus.

- He give us boldness to take a stand for what we believe.

- He give us boldness to share the gospel.

- He give us boldness to defend those that are being hurt.

- He give us boldness to tell the truth.

- He give us boldness to not be ashamed that we are Christians. (praying in public, etc).

We can't simply determine to be bold. We can't muster up boldness on our own. Instead, we must rely on God's power to give us the boldness we need in our Christian lives.

CRAFT—Paul Mini Activity Book

Supplies

Life of Paul mini activity book printable from Ministry Resource download

Instructions

1. Print off the mini activity book pages.
2. Cut each page in half to make a 8.5 x 5.5 page.
3. Cut each page in half again to make a 5.5 x 4.25 page.
4. Fold in half.
5. Using a hole punch, punch three holes. Cut three pieces of yarn approximately four inches. Tie each piece of the yarn in a knot to complete the book.

Application

As students complete the mini activity book at home or in class, encourage them to remember the boldness God gave Paul and to ask God for that same boldness to live for Him.

ADDITIONAL RESOURCES

Find the following items on the Ministry Resource download:

- Coloring Page (for younger children)
- Activity Page (for older children)
- Student Take-Home Paper
- PowerPoint Presentation

Note for Next Week:

Next week's craft requires individual photos of your students. You may want to take these photos this week, so you have time to print and assemble them before the next class time.

Suggested Classroom Schedule

Before Class	Complete attendance record. Provide students with coloring pages/activity pages.
Opening	Welcome
Prayer	Prayer requests and praise reports from the children
Song Time	
Object Lesson	Pattern of Good Behavior
Memory Verse	1 Timothy 4:12
Song Time	
Bible Lesson	Timothy
Application/Invitation	Help saved students apply lesson. Invite unsaved students to receive Christ.
Snack	Sandal Cookies
Review Game/ Questions	
Craft	Timothy Door Hanger
Closing	Give announcements and pray. Distribute take-home papers.

Lesson Twelve Overview

Timothy
Theme—Walking with God in Youth

Scripture
Acts 16:1-5

Memory Verse
1 Timothy 4:12—"*Let no man despise thy youth; but be thou an example of the believers, in word, in conversation, in charity, in spirit, in faith, in purity.*"

Lesson Outline
Introducing the Story
The man in today's true story from the Bible had an important decision to make early in his childhood—a decision many people have to make. We're going to see the differences his decisions made in his life—and in our lives today.

Telling the Story
1. **Timothy's Family** (*Acts 16:1*)
2. **Lois and Eunice Teach Timothy the Scriptures**
    (*2 Timothy 3:15*) —Flashcard 12.1
3. **Timothy Chooses** (*Acts 16:1*)
    —*Flashcard 12.2*
4. **Timothy Is Chosen** (*Acts 16:2-5*)
    —*Flashcard 12.3*

Applying the Story
The choices Timothy had to make as a young boy are just like yours. Once you have trusted Jesus as your Saviour, you have another choice to make—the same one Timothy had to make: Will you walk with the Lord and live for him, or will you follow the ways of the people around you?

LESSON TWELVE

(12) Timothy

Theme: Walking with God in Youth

TEACHER'S CHECKLIST

- ❏ Read Acts 16:1–5; 1 Timothy, 2 Timothy 1:1–5: 3:10–15.
- ❏ Study Lesson Twelve.
- ❏ Flash cards 12.1–12.3.
- ❏ Purchase snack—Sandal Cookies.
- ❏ Gather for "Use an Object"—ice cream containers.
- ❏ Gather for "Draw it!"—dry-erase marker and pens for students.
- ❏ Gather for review game—30 envelopes, one marker, candy, point cards from the Ministry Resource download.
- ❏ Gather for object lesson—sewing pattern.
- ❏ Gather for craft—"I Will Walk with God" printable from Ministry Resource download, student photos, yarn, hole punch.
- ❏ Print for review game—point cards from the Ministry Resource download.
- ❏ Print Memory Verse Flashcards from the Ministry Resource download.
- ❏ Print for craft—"I Will Walk with God" printable from Ministry Resource download.
- ❏ Print and duplicate Coloring Pages or Activity Pages on the Ministry Resource download (one per student).
- ❏ Print and duplicate Take-Home Paper on the Ministry Resource download (one per student).

SNACK SUGGESTION

Sandal Cookies
Purchase Nutter Butters cookies and with frosting, add two lines to create flip flop straps. At the top to the sandal, where the flip flop straps meet, you can add a decorative embellishment.

SCRIPTURES

Acts 16:1–5

1 Then came he to Derbe and Lystra: and, behold, a certain disciple was there, named Timotheus, the son of a certain woman, which was a Jewess, and believed; but his father was a Greek:

2 Which was well reported of by the brethren that were at Lystra and Iconium.

MEMORY VERSE

1 Timothy 4:12
"Let no man despise thy youth; but be thou an example of the believers, in word, in conversation, in charity, in spirit, in faith, in purity."

3 Him would Paul have to go forth with him; and took and circumcised him because of the Jews which were in those quarters: for they knew all that his father was a Greek.

4 And as they went through the cities, they delivered them the decrees for to keep, that were ordained of the apostles and elders which were at Jerusalem.

5 And so were the churches established in the faith, and increased in number daily.

USE AN OBJECT

Bring in empty ice cream containers or print ice cream pictures from the Ministry Resource download. Ask the students what ice cream they would choose if given the choice. (Variation: Consider bringing ice cream with varying flavors to class and allowing the students to choose what flavor they would like to enjoy for their snack.)

BIBLE LESSON

Introducing the Story

What choices can you think of that you have to make regularly—sometimes every day?

- What will we eat?
- How will we spend our time?
- What will we wear?
- Where will we go?
- How will we treat our brothers and sisters?
- How will we respond to someone else's unkindness?

Some choices make a difference for that moment; and, although they are important, they don't have as much impact on the rest of our lives as other choices.

- Should I eat another cookie?
- Should I do my math or history homework first?
- Should I play soccer or tennis?

Some choices make a difference for the rest of our lives—they shape our lives, or they have a part in shaping someone else's life.

- Should I obey my parents, or do what my friends are doing?
- Should I copy my classmate's test answers, or should I just put down the answers I know and leave the rest blank?
- Should I share the gospel with my friend, or should we just do fun stuff together and not talk about religion?
- Should I read the Bible first thing in the morning, or should I play a game?

The biggest, most life-changing decision we will ever make is: Should I trust Jesus and His sacrifice on the cross to pay for my sins, or should I go my own way?

The man in today's true story from the Bible had another decision to make early in his childhood—a decision many people have to make. You see, Timothy's mother believed in the one true God of Heaven, and his father didn't. We're going to see the differences his decision (as to whose beliefs he would follow) made for him, and for all of us today.

THE STORY

1. Timothy's Family (Acts 16:1)

Our story really begins with Timothy's grandmother, Lois, because she was a major part of Timothy's life—she may even have lived in the same home as Timothy. Lois was a Jewish woman who believed in God and trusted the Bible that one day God would send the Messiah—the Saviour who would pay the price for her sins.

Lois carefully studied and learned the Old Testament. It's the only part of the Bible that was written then, as the New Testament begins with the birth of Jesus; and He hadn't yet been born.

When Lois married and had a daughter of her own, she taught her daughter, Eunice, the Old Testament Scriptures. They studied them faithfully, and both Lois and Eunice looked forward to the day the Messiah would come.

Lois and Eunice lived in the city of Lystra, which is in present day Turkey. Most of the people who lived around them were Greeks, who didn't know or worship the true God of Heaven.

Somewhere in her late teenage or young adult years, Eunice, sadly, married a man who didn't believe in the true God.

2 Corinthians 6:14

14 Be ye not unequally yoked together with unbelievers: for what fellowship hath righteousness with unrighteousness? and what communion hath light with darkness?

He was a Greek who likely worshiped the false gods of his people. The Bible doesn't give us his name.

Eunice and her husband had a son, Timothy. It's hard for a Christian mother to raise her child to know the Lord when the child's father doesn't know the Lord. What would Eunice do?

DRAW IT!

LOIS

DRAW IT!

EUNICE

DRAW IT!

GREEK MAN

DRAW IT!

TIMOTHY

DRAW IT!

WHAT WOULD EUNICE DO?

DRAW IT!

WISE UNTO SALVATION

2. Lois and Eunice Teach Timothy the Scriptures (2 Timothy 3:15)

Eunice made a decision. "I'm going to teach Timothy the truth; I'm going to teach him the Scriptures. If I teach him God's Word, there is so much more hope that Timothy will one day trust in the Messiah. If he doesn't trust in the Messiah, he will spend forever in the place the Bible calls Hell."

So Eunice, with the help of her mother Lois, diligently taught the Scriptures to Timothy. They knew that if he knew the Scriptures, he would be likely to trust the Messiah when He came.

2 Timothy 3:15

15 And that from a child thou hast known the holy scriptures, which are able to make thee wise unto salvation through faith which is in Christ Jesus.

Together, Lois and Eunice set out to do everything they could to share the Lord with Timothy. They told him how God had worked in the lives of the Jewish people in the Old Testament. They knew Timothy had a choice to make in his life, and they wanted Timothy to know God and His greatness. "If Timothy knows how wonderful God is," they said, "he will surely trust in Him and follow the Messiah."

Psalm 78:5–7

5 For he established a testimony in Jacob, and appointed a law in Israel, which he commanded our fathers, that they should make them known to their children:

6 That the generation to come might know them, even the children which should be born; who should arise and declare them to their children:

7 That they might set their hope in God, and not forget the works of God, but keep his commandments:

Flash Card 12.1

Timothy listened to the stories his mom and grandma told him from the Old Testament:

- They taught him that God created the world—out of nothing—in six days. He made everything there is, including the first man and woman, Adam and Eve.

Adam and Eve chose to sin—to disobey God, and go their own way—and because of this, death came into the world. That's what God had warned them would happen.

God promised to send the Messiah—a Saviour to pay the price for our sins so we wouldn't have to suffer eternal death in a place the Bible calls Hell. Those who trust in the Messiah will have their sins forgiven, and they will be given eternal life. They will get to live in Heaven with God after they die!

- They told him about Noah and the ark, and how God saved Noah's family through their faith from a great flood that destroyed the rest of the world.

- They taught him about Moses, and God using him to lead millions of Israelite people through the wilderness to a land He promised to give them. They told him of the miracles God did through Moses, and how God provided for the needs of those millions of people for forty years in the wilderness.

- They told him about King David, Shadrach, Meshach, Abednego, and Daniel—who all chose to walk with and serve the Lord.

- They told him about the prophets God sent to tell what God would do in the future and to turn the hearts of the people to the Lord.

- Along with these and many other wonderful things God did in the Bible for His people, they told Timothy about the law God had given. God instructed us to keep the law, but He knew that none of us would be able to keep every bit of the law, so He promised to send a Saviour to pay for sin.

Day after day, year after year, Lois and Eunice taught the Scriptures to Timothy.

3. Timothy Chooses (Acts 16:1)

Timothy had a choice: who would he believe—the God of his mother and grandmother, or the gods of his dad and the people around him? Timothy may have lived in a single parent home—maybe his dad had died or maybe he just didn't live there. The Bible only mentions that he was a Greek.

"Mom and Grandma are different than the other people of Lystra," Timothy thought. "What they believe makes a difference in their lives. Their love for God shows in their love for other people. They have peace in their

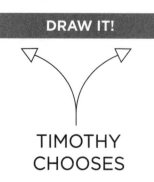

DRAW IT!

TIMOTHY CHOOSES

hearts. They aren't looking for something to fill their lives, because their lives are full of love for God. He must be the true God."

While Timothy was still young, some missionaries—Paul, Barnabas, and John Mark—came to Lystra, preaching the gospel.

"The Messiah has come," they preached. "We are all sinners, and the penalty for sin is death and hell. But Jesus Christ, God the Son, was born of a virgin, died on the cross, and rose again from the dead so we wouldn't have to pay for our own sins. You see, He paid the price for us. Trust Him as your Saviour."

Lois, Eunice, and Timothy heard for the first time that the Messiah had already come. It may have been that very day, or it may have been shortly afterward, but all three of them trusted in Jesus as their Saviour from sin!

Timothy continued to study the Scriptures. Now that he was God's child, he wanted more than ever to know Him and to walk with Him.

DRAW IT!

Flash Card 12.2

John 1:12

12 But as many as received him, to them gave he power to become the sons of God, even to them that believe on his name:

Now that Timothy was a Christian, he had another decision to make. Would he continue walking with God, or would he just be glad he no longer would have to go to Hell when he died, and live his life like the people around him?

Sometimes the world around him looked like more fun. It would be easier to live like everyone else—to go the places they went and do the things they did. But Timothy knew that wasn't what he wanted.

The Lord Jesus Christ had paid the price Timothy owed for his sin when He died on the cross. "He gave everything for me," Timothy thought. "I want to know and live for the Lord Who died for me."

And that's the choice Timothy made. The Lord became everything to him. He spent more time than ever studying the Scriptures and talking to the Lord in prayer. And his Christianity didn't just stay in his heart—it showed on the outside!

Everyone knew Timothy was a Christian. His love for the Lord shone in everything he said and did. He obeyed his parents. He helped his neighbors. His word could be trusted, because he was known for telling the truth. He shared the gospel. He was kind and generous. He trusted in God, and he wasn't ashamed to say he believed in the God of the Bible.

4. Timothy Is Chosen (Acts 16:2–5)

Paul returned to Timothy's city of Lystra, and he was looking for a faithful man to travel with him and help him as he shared the gospel with those who didn't know the Lord.

"We know just who you're looking for," said the Christians at Lystra. "We have in our church a young man named Timothy. He has an amazing testimony and reputation. We have watched him. He really lives what he says he believes. He is honest and hard-working. He loves the Lord with all his heart. He would be exactly what you need, Paul."

When Paul met Timothy, Eunice, and Lois, he knew Timothy would be just right for the job. He could see that Timothy had chosen to follow the Lord in every area of life. "Will you come with me?" Paul asked.

Paul became like a father to Timothy, calling him son, and teaching him how to serve the Lord. Timothy learned from watching Paul and from the things Paul taught him.

That was the beginning of many trips Paul and Timothy took together, sharing the gospel and starting churches.

Eventually Paul left Timothy to lead the church they began in the city of Ephesus, and he went on to other places. Paul was put into prison for preaching the gospel, and he wrote letters to Timothy, teaching Timothy how to lead the church.

DRAW IT!

PAUL	☐
TIMOTHY	

"I know you are young," Paul wrote, "but don't let people have a low opinion of you just because you are young. Be an example of what a believer should be (1 Timothy 4:12). Be an example:

- in what you say
- in what you do
- in your love
- in your attitude
- in your faith
- in your pure and holy walk with the Lord

Paul wrote this to Timothy because he knew Timothy had done all this since he was young. He knew Timothy was already an example of what a Christian should be, and he wanted to remind him to keep it up.

"But Timothy, my son, it won't always be easy to follow the Lord. You need to be strong as you go through hard times—be a good soldier for the Lord!" (2 Timothy 2:3).

The letters Paul wrote to Timothy are now part of the Bible I hold in my hand—the books of first and second Timothy.

APPLYING THE STORY

Think about your family—about your life. Right now, in your own mind, think about how your life is like, or unlike, Timothy's life. Do both your parents believe in the Lord and trust Jesus as their Saviour? Does only one of your parents trust Jesus? Do neither of your parents trust Him?

Do you live with both of your parents, or just one of them? Or maybe neither of them—maybe you live with your grandparents, with other relatives, or in a foster home.

Is it hard for you to know whether you should choose to trust the Lord or choose to follow the way of your unsaved family member or others around you?

The choices Timothy had to make were just like yours. Even as a boy, he had to choose.

Sometimes we think we'll wait until later to trust Jesus, thinking we won't decide right now. But that really is a decision. That is a decision not to trust Him. Oh, you might decide to trust Him later on, but you can't really be sure you will have the opportunity.

Timothy trusted Him as his Saviour while he was still a boy.

And, once you have trusted Jesus as your Saviour, you have another choice to make—the same one Timothy had to make: Will you follow the Lord and live for him, or will you follow the ways of the people around you? Timothy chose to follow the Lord, even though he was very young.

That kept Timothy from having to make that decision later on in life—after he had already lived according to the ways of the people who didn't know God.

Have you heard the saying, "You can't teach an old dog new tricks"? That means it's harder to unlearn the bad that comes into your life than it is to start out from the beginning learning the good.

Because Timothy chose to walk with God early in his life, his life was full of the blessings of God:

- God spoke to him every day through the Bible.

- He had great family relationships because he followed God's directions for living.

- People trusted him because he had a reputation for speaking the truth.

- He knew the joy of giving to others for the Lord.

- He knew all his money came to him honestly through hard work.

- His mind was pure because he had chosen to think about and look at things that helped him walk more closely with the Lord.

Philippians 4:8

8   Finally, brethren, whatsoever things are true, whatsoever things are honest, whatsoever things are just, whatsoever things are pure, whatsoever things are lovely, whatsoever things are of good report; if there be any virtue, and if there be any praise, think on these things.

Because Timothy chose to walk with God early in life, he wasn't full of regrets:

- He didn't have to wish he hadn't gotten drunk and done things he wished he never had.

- He didn't have to wish he hadn't beaten his wife.

- He didn't have to wish he wasn't in jail for selling drugs.

- He didn't have to wish he hadn't robbed the store down the street.

- He didn't have to wish he could get awful pictures and thoughts out of his mind.

- He didn't have to wish people wouldn't distrust him because he lied so much.

Last week we learned about Paul, the man who had persecuted Christians—imprisoning and killing them—before he became a Christian. He trusted the Lord, and God used him in wonderful ways to share the gospel. He even shared it in Timothy's city!

Timothy didn't have the kind of regrets Paul had. His mind was clean and pure and full of the Scriptures.

God can, and does, use both kinds of people in wonderful, miraculous ways. He is the God of grace!

But, many people who didn't get saved until later in life give testimony that they wish they had trusted the Lord at a young age and walked with God all their lives.

You are still young, and you have the choice before you right now. You don't have to say at the end of your life, "I wish I had…."

REVIEW GAME/QUESTIONS

Find the Match

Materials Needed

30 envelopes—1 set of 3 for each question

Marker

Point cards from the Ministry Resource download

Small candy or treat

Set Up

Print and cut the point cards. Then place them inside the envelopes, making sure to include one card of each point range (0 points, 1–50 points, 50–100 points) with in each set of three envelopes.

Label the envelopes with the numbers: 1, 2, 3 for each set

Arrange the envelopes (on the board or pocket chart), so that they are in ten sets of three (one set for each review question.)

Playing the Game

Divide the class into two teams and ask the review questions. When a student answers correctly, he may choose an envelope from the set of three on the board. His team is awarded the points that he selects from his envelope. The team with the most points at the end of the game wins.

Variation: The envelope containing point cards ranging from 1–50 can be replaced with a small candy or treat. This would mean that one envelope would offer no reward, one would offer a personal treat, and one would offer team points.

1. What is the biggest and most life-changing decision you will ever make?
   Answer: Trusting Jesus as your Saviour

2. What were the names of Timothy's grandmother and mother?
   Answer: Grandmother—Lois; mother—Eunice

3. What do we know about Timothy's dad?
   Answer: He was a Greek; didn't know the Lord

4. What choice did Lois (Timothy's mother) have to make?
   Answer: She chose to teach Timothy God's Word, when his father believed in other gods.

5. Why did Lois and Eunice teach Timothy the Old Testament?
   Answer: They knew that if Timothy knew God's Word, he would be more likely to accept the Messiah when He came.

6. What choice did Timothy have to make? What choice did he make?
   Answer: He had to choose whether to follow his grandmother and mother's true God, or to follow the false gods of his father. He chose to follow and believe the one true God.

7. What missionary, who became like a father to Timothy, did Timothy travel with, learn from, and help?
   Answer: Paul

8. What job did Paul give Timothy to do after Paul left him?
   Answer: Timothy became the leader of the church in Ephesus.

9. What is the choice that all of us who have already trusted Jesus as Saviour must make?
   Answer: We must decide if we will follow the Lord and live for Him, or if we will follow the ways of the people around us.

10. What are some of the ways that God blessed Timothy after he chose to walk with God?
    Answer: God spoke to him every day through the Bible, he had great family relationships because He followed God's directions for living, people trusted him because they knew he would tell the truth, he knew the joy of giving to others for the Lord, he knew all his money came to him honestly, and his mind was pure because he had chosen to think about and look at things that helped him walk more closely with the Lord.

Teaching the Memory Verse

1 Timothy 4:12

12 Let no man despise thy youth; but be thou an example of the believers, in word, in conversation, in charity, in spirit, in faith, in purity.

Materials Needed

Memory Verse Flashcards from the Ministry Resource download

Teaching the Verse

Recite the verse together several times as a class. Then, call a student up to the front who will lead the class by example in saying the verse. The student can choose how the verse will be spoken, and the other students can follow the example. Some example ideas include:

- Reading the verse slowly
- Reading the verse loudly
- Saying the verse while turning around in a circle
- Reading the verse while laughing

OBJECT LESSON— Pattern of Good Behavior

Materials Needed

Sewing pattern

Lesson

Bring a sewing pattern to class and pull out the different pieces of the pattern, showing the sleeves, pant legs, etc. A sewing pattern provides a template or example for the finished product.

Application

God wanted Timothy to be an example to the believers—a pattern of good works, faith, and charity. God wants us to be an example, too. He wants us to choose to be a pattern of good behavior as children, so we can continue to walk with Him as adults.

CRAFT—Timothy Door Hanger

Supplies

"I Will Walk with God" printable from
    Ministry Resource download
Student photos
Yarn
Hole punch

Instructions

1. Print "I Will Walk with God" template for each student.
2. Take a photo of each student, print, and glue to the center of the printable.
3. Hole punch one hole on the top right and top left of the printable.
4. Tie one piece of yarn to each side.

Application

Hang this reminder on your bedroom door, so it can remind you to walk with God as you pass by it each day!

ADDITIONAL RESOURCES

Find the following items on the Ministry Resource download:

*   Coloring Page (for younger children)
*   Activity Page (for older children)
*   Student Take-Home Paper
*   PowerPoint Presentation

Suggested Classroom Schedule

Before Class	Complete attendance record. Provide students with coloring pages/activity pages.	
Opening	Welcome	
Prayer	Prayer requests and praise reports from the children	
Song Time		
Memory Verse	1 Peter 4:9	
Song Time		
Object Lesson	Pineapples & Hospitality	
Bible Lesson	Lydia	
Application/Invitation	Help saved students apply lesson. Invite unsaved students to receive Christ.	
Snack	Purple Popcorn	
Review Game/ Questions		
Craft	Lydia Placemat	
Closing	Give announcements and pray. Distribute take-home papers.	

Lesson Thirteen Overview

Lydia
Theme—Hospitality

Scripture
Acts 16:13–14

Memory Verse
1 Peter 4:9—*"Use hospitality one to another without grudging."*

Lesson Outline
Introducing the Story
Hospitality is something that can, and should, be part of all our lives—from the youngest of us to the oldest. Today's true story from the Bible will give us a picture of what real hospitality looks like, and how God used the hospitality of one woman to change the world.

Telling the Story
1. **Lydia's Early Years** *(Acts 16:14)*
   —*Flashcard 13.1*

2. **Paul called to Macedonia** *(Acts 16:1-12)*
   —*Flashcard 13.2*

3. **Lydia's Conversion** *(Acts 16:13-14)*

4. **Lydia Becomes a Disciple** *(Acts 16:15; 40)*
   —*Flashcard 13.3*

Applying the Story
Hospitality is really opening your heart and all you have to others. Hospitality is realizing that all you have has been given to you by God, and using it for His purposes. Hospitality is a work of God through you.

Lydia

Theme: Hospitality

TEACHER'S CHECKLIST

- ❏ Read Acts 16:13–14.
- ❏ Study Lesson Thirteen.
- ❏ Flash cards 13.1–13.3.
- ❏ Prepare snack— Purple Popcorn.
- ❏ Gather for "Use an Object"—bolt or yard of purple material.
- ❏ Gather for object lesson—Whole pineapple, Pineapple chunks, toothpicks.
- ❏ Gather for review game—6 inch craft test tubes, food dye, craft paint and brush, pitcher of water, prizes for winners.
- ❏ Gather for teaching the memory verse—sticker magnets, Memory Verse Flashcards and Pineapple Verse Cards from the Ministry Resource download.
- ❏ Gather for craft—Lydia placemat printable from Ministry Resource download, individual student photos, contact paper.
- ❏ Print for teaching the verse—Memory Verse Flashcards and Pineapple Verse Cards from the Ministry Resource download.
- ❏ Pring for craft—Lydia placemat printable from Ministry Resource download.
- ❏ Print and duplicate Coloring Pages or Activity Pages on the Ministry Resource download (one per student).
- ❏ Print and duplicate Take-Home Paper on the Ministry Resource download (one per student).

SNACK SUGGESTION

Purple Popcorn
Pop popcorn and place in a large bowl or spread evenly onto wax paper. Melt white chocolate melting discs (1lb package for 8 bags of popcorn) and stir in purple food coloring. Depending on the desired amount of white chocolate, either stir the chocolate and popcorn together in a large bowl or drizzle the purple-colored chocolate over the popcorn located on the wax paper. Allow to cool and portion small amounts for easy distribution in class.

MEMORY VERSE

1 Peter 4:9
"Use hospitality one to another without grudging."

SCRIPTURES

Acts 16:13–14

13 And on the sabbath we went out of the city by a river side, where prayer was wont to be made; and we sat down, and spake unto the women which resorted thither.

14 And a certain woman named Lydia, a seller of purple, of the city of Thyatira, which worshipped God, heard us: whose heart the Lord opened, that she attended unto the things which were spoken of Paul.

Introducing the Story

Hospitality is a word that describes something we usually think of as a nice thing to do. What do you picture when you think of hospitality? (Allow students to respond.)

We may think of a family who invites people over to their home for Sunday dinner. Or we might think of someone who often has company over for activities. Or maybe it's someone who has relatives spend the night when they are visiting. We usually think of hospitality as being willing to entertain guests—especially our friends and family—in our homes.

Hospitality might seem like something that doesn't apply much to your lives right now, since you aren't the decision-maker for what goes on in your home.

The truth is, hospitality is something that can, and should, be part of all our lives—from the youngest of us to the oldest. In fact, hospitality is something that God instructs all Christians to develop in their lives.

1 Peter 4:9
9 Use hospitality one to another without grudging.

Grudging simply means "unwillingly" or "reluctantly." It means you don't want to do the thing you are asked to do. So, God tells us to use hospitality toward others with happy hearts.

Today's true story from the Bible will give us a picture of what real hospitality looks like, and how God used the hospitality of one woman to change the world.

THE STORY

1. Lydia's Early Years (Acts 16:14)

Lydia was born in the busy city of Thyatira, in what is now the country of Turkey. The people of Thyatira were idol worshipers who didn't know the true God who created the world.

In Thyatira were temples built to honor idols, such as the sun god. Worshipers of these false gods would go to the temple and give gifts and offer sacrifices to these idols, hoping the idols would give them success in life.

This is all Lydia knew. As she watched the people worship their false idols, she wondered, "Is this really all there is to life? Do these idols really help people?"

As Lydia grew, she became interested in the trade Thyatira was famous for—making a beautiful purple/red dye that was richer in color than anyone else knew how to make.

"I love that beautiful color," Lydia thought. She loved to watch the dye workers as they collected thousands and thousands of little shellfish, called murex. From the throat of each shellfish, they would extract a drop of the precious fluid that would be turned into purple dye. When they had enough of the fluid, they would place it on wool, which turned the dye a blue color. Then, they set the fluid out in the sunlight, where it would turn first green, then purple, and, finally, a beautiful deep crimson color. This dye, which was called purple, was very expensive and used by only royalty and very wealthy people.

"I could do that," Lydia thought, and she set about learning how to make the dye. Did Lydia ever marry and have children? We don't know, but we do know that she became a very successful businesswoman, selling the purple to other countries.

As she went about her business, she finally moved across the Aegean Sea to the city of Philippi in Macedonia, in what is now southern Europe.

2. Paul Called to Macedonia (Acts 16:1–12)

The missionaries Paul and Timothy, along with Silas and Luke, were traveling from city to city in Asia. As they preached and taught, they started new churches in every city where people trusted in Jesus as their Saviour from sin.

One night after they had gone to bed, Paul saw a vision. A man from Macedonia stood, calling to him, "Come over into Macedonia, and help us."

"There's no question," Paul thought. "The Lord is calling us further than I imagined He would. He is calling us to go to Macedonia to preach the gospel to those who have never heard the good news about Jesus."

So, Paul, Timothy, Silas, and Luke (Paul's doctor and the godly writer of the book of Acts) immediately found a ship sailing to Macedonia. As they sailed, they must have been full of excitement, wondering what God would do and to whom God would lead them in Macedonia.

Shortly after they landed in Macedonia, they made the ten mile journey to Philippi, the largest city in that part of Macedonia.

There was no one to welcome them to Philippi—no one inviting them to spend the night in their home or offering them a meal. But they knew God had called them there, and so they stayed.

USE AN OBJECT

Bring in a bolt or yard of purple cloth to display as you teach.

Flash Card 13.1

TEACHER'S NOTE

Depending on the age and attention span of your students, you may wish to share the following review from past lessons.

The apostle Paul, remember, had been saved after years of cruelly persecuting Christians. Timothy was saved at a young age, and Paul became like a father to Timothy, as Timothy became Paul's companion and helper.

Most of the people living in Philippi—in all of Macedonia, actually—were Greeks (also called Gentiles), who worshiped false idols. The work the missionaries had before them, preaching to all these idol worshipers, was going to be extremely hard.

But Gentiles were not the only ones living in Philippi. There were a few Jews who now made their home in Philippi; and as these Jews shared stories of the true God and His power and the mighty works He had done, a few of the Greeks turned away from their idols and believed in the God of the Bible.

1 Thessalonians 1:9

9   For they themselves shew of us what manner of entering in we had unto you, and how ye turned to God from idols to serve the living and true God;

Now, these Greeks became Jews, but that doesn't mean they became Christians. A Christian is someone who has trusted in Jesus Christ as his Saviour and follows Him. But, at the time Paul received the vision to go to Macedonia, the Jews in Macedonia didn't know that the Messiah (Jesus) had come. They hadn't heard that He had been crucified and risen from the dead to pay for their sins. They still followed the law of the Old Testament, and they still waited for the Messiah to come.

Flash Card 13.2 ▶

The city of Philippi was full of idol worship. In fact, there were so few Jews living in Philippi that they didn't even have a synagogue to worship in.

In the past, when Paul had gone into a city, he would immediately find the synagogue, and begin preaching the gospel—that Jesus died on the cross to pay for our sins, was buried, and rose again the third day; and those who trust Him as their Saviour from sin would become God's children and have eternal life.

John 1:12

12   But as many as received him, to them gave he power to become the sons of God, even to them that believe on his name:

Since there was no synagogue, Paul began asking around. "Where do the Jews meet?"

"There's a place down by the riverside," someone answered. "If you go there on Saturday, you will find them meeting for prayer."

3. Lydia's Conversion (Acts 16:13–14)

When Paul and the others got to the riverside, they found a small group of women meeting for prayer. "Hmm…interesting that God would send us all the way to Macedonia to speak to this small group of women," they must have thought. "I wonder what He plans to do here."

But this is where God had sent them, and Paul preached the gospel to these few women, just as if they had been a synagogue full of listeners.

One of these women at the river was Lydia. Through her business, Lydia had met all kinds of people—some of them Jews. As she had developed relationships with the Jews, she listened to their stories about God. She learned about His creation of the world, sin coming into the world, and God promising a Messiah to save us from our sins. Lydia believed. "There is only one true God," she realized. "I am going to worship Him. I have decided to become a Jew."

Lydia met with the other Jewish women every Sabbath day for prayer and worship. And, although all the Greeks around her went on with business as usual on the Sabbath day, Lydia stopped her work and worshiped the Lord. The Greeks must have thought these Jews were very strange.

Lydia listened carefully to everything Paul said. This was exactly what Lydia was waiting to hear—the Messiah had come! Paul's words were not just the words of a preacher—they were *God's* words. Through Paul's preaching God's Word, and Lydia's listening to it, God opened Lydia's heart; and she trusted in Jesus.

Hebrews 4:12

12 For the word of God is quick, and powerful, and sharper than any twoedged sword, piercing even to the dividing asunder of soul and spirit, and of the joints and marrow, and is a discerner of the thoughts and intents of the heart.

4. Lydia Becomes a Disciple (Acts 16:15; 40)

Paul not only taught the women to trust Jesus for salvation, but he taught them to be baptized after they trusted Jesus.

Matthew 28:19

19 Go ye therefore, and teach all nations, baptizing them in the name of the Father, and of the Son, and of the Holy Ghost:

Flash Card 13.3 ▶

Lydia's heart was immediately changed when she trusted in Jesus. She wanted to obey everything the Lord told her to do. She was gladly baptized to show that she was a follower of Christ.

"I want to learn all I can," Lydia told Paul. "Please, if you believe I am sincere, come stay in my home."

"We really couldn't do that," the missionaries argued. "Look, there are so many of us—we wouldn't expect you to provide for so many of us."

"No, please, I insist. Come—stay in my home."

Paul, Silas, Timothy, and Luke did stay in Lydia's home. From her home they went out into the city every day to preach the gospel. At night they returned to Lydia's house, where they taught Lydia and other Christians how to grow in the Lord.

The missionaries had trials in Philippi. Not everyone wanted to hear the gospel. Many people were afraid they would lose the money they earned from fortune telling and other types of demon worship, if people believed the gospel.

1 Timothy 6:10

10 For the love of money is the root of all evil: which while some coveted after, they have erred from the faith, and pierced themselves through with many sorrows.

Paul and Silas were accused of speaking against the culture and government of Philippi, and they were beaten and thrown into prison. When they were released, the city officials asked them to leave Philippi.

Paul and Silas returned to Lydia's house, where Christians were meeting for prayer and studying God's Word. What had started with the salvation of one woman, was now a group of people who loved and worshiped the Lord Jesus Christ—and would soon become the church at Philippi!

God used the salvation, and the hospitality that resulted from that salvation, of one woman to be the start of the very first Christian church in Europe!

APPLYING THE STORY

As soon as Lydia was saved, she showed hospitality. God had actually prepared and enabled Lydia to be able to show the kind of hospitality He planned for her to show. He allowed her to have a successful business so she could afford to meet the missionaries' needs. He allowed her to move from Thyatira to Philippi, where she would meet Paul and the other missionaries when they first came to

Europe. He allowed her to own a home large enough to house the missionaries and provide a place where they could teach new believers to grow in the Lord.

The true definition of hospitality is "the act or practice of receiving and entertaining strangers or guests without reward, or with kind and generous liberality" (Webster's 1828 Dictionary of the English Language). It means we show warmth, friendliness, and kindness to others. In the original Greek language of the New Testament, it specifically meant "brotherly love shown to strangers."

That gives us a little different picture of hospitality than we usually think of—brotherly love shown to strangers! It's sometimes not too difficult to think of showing love and kindness to those we know and feel comfortable with—but to strangers?!

Hebrews 13:2

2   Be not forgetful to entertain strangers: for thereby some have entertained angels unawares.

Strangers were very important in the Jews' understanding of their history. Many years earlier, the Jews moved into Egypt, and over the course of time, the Egyptians made them into slaves. The Jews were forced to do more work than it was possible to do in a day, and they were beaten when they couldn't meet the goals set before them. They were strangers living in a land of Egyptians, and their lives were very, very hard.

After the Jews were delivered from Egypt and the bondage of slavery, God told them often to remember what it was like to be strangers in Egypt. He wanted them to remember, so they would treat strangers with love and kindness.

Exodus 23:9

9   Also thou shalt not oppress a stranger: for ye know the heart of a stranger, seeing ye were strangers in the land of Egypt.

Deuteronomy 10:19

19   Love ye therefore the stranger: for ye were strangers in the land of Egypt.

That's exactly what Lydia did. Before that day at the river, Lydia had never met the missionaries; yet, when she got saved, she invited them to her home. This invitation was not just for a meal, but to stay as long as they were in Philippi.

TEACHER'S TIP

Write the word, *hospitality*, on the board. Ask the students if they see another word hidden inside this word. The word *hospital* is part of the word *hospitality*. Originally, hospitals began as a place to provide hospitality and accommodations for people. As time went on, the medical treatments became more prominent in hospitals and the meaning of the word *hospital* is now slightly different than it once was. Both words have the connotation of kindness, generosity, and care.

And, as more people trusted Jesus, they were welcomed into Lydia's home to be taught to grow in the Lord.

What does hospitality mean in the life of a _____ year old? (Teacher, fill in the blank with the ages of your students.)

Since you don't usually make decisions about who will come over for lunch, what meal will be prepared, and whether you will invite them to spend the night, (those things are usually up to your parents,) how can you show hospitality to others? (Allow students to respond.)

Hospitality is really opening your heart and all you have to others. Hospitality is realizing that all you have has been given to you by God, and using it for His purposes. Hospitality is a work of God through you.

What has God given you that you can use for others?

> **TEACHER'S NOTE**
>
> Be sure to remind your students that hospitality is to encourage others and draw them to the Lord. We need to be careful as we minister to those who don't know the Lord or who are not walking with Him, that we ourselves are not influenced by them, rather than influencing them for Christ. This is a caution Christians always need to heed.

- Do you have salvation? You can share the gospel with someone who is lost. This is the ultimate hospitality—sharing the gospel with someone who doesn't know the Lord.

- Do you have friends? You can invite someone who is lonely to spend time with you and your friends, doing whatever you are doing.

- Do you have a church? You can invite someone who doesn't go to church to come with you on Sunday.

- Do you have a lunch? You can share it with someone who has forgotten theirs, or who just doesn't have one.

- Do you have an allowance or other money? You can purchase a gift or something someone needs that will encourage their hearts.

- Do you have loving parents or others who have spoken kind words to you? You can speak those same words of kindness to others.

- Do you have a smile? A smile is a free gift you can give to everyone. Often a smile is just what a discouraged person needs to lift their spirits.

- Do you have the sense of hearing? You can listen to someone who has burdens on their heart.

- Do you have wisdom from the Lord? You can share it with someone who has a decision to make.

- Do you have permission from your parents to have people over to your home? You can invite someone who is lonely.

- Have you ever been encouraged by a cheerful card when you were sick (or even just wished someone would send you a card?) You can send a cheerful card to someone who is sick.

- Can you bake? You could bake treats and take them to a nursing home and share them with the elderly people you visit.

We don't need to be wealthy or grown up to show hospitality—we just need a heart to serve Jesus. Hospitality is really sharing with others the grace God has shown to you.

Matthew 25:35–36

35 For I was an hungered, and ye gave me meat: I was thirsty, and ye gave me drink: I was a stranger, and ye took me in:

36 Naked, and ye clothed me: I was sick, and ye visited me: I was in prison, and ye came unto me.

Remember, God used one woman's hospitality to be the start of Europe's first church. Imagine what He could do through you!

REVIEW GAME/QUESTIONS

Materials Needed
6 inch craft test tubes with cap (available at amazon.com or a local craft store)
Different colors of food dye (at least one color should be purple)
Craft paint and brush
Pitcher or bottle of water
Prizes for winners

Set up
Using the craft paint, paint the bottom portion of the outside of each test tube a dark color, so that the dye is hidden inside. (Water bottles can be used in place of test tubes.)

When the paint has dried, fill each test tube with a different drop of food coloring, ensuring that at least one tube contains purple dye.

Playing the Game
Ask a review question. When the student answers correctly, allow him to come to the front and pour water in a tube, revealing the color inside.

Variation One: Divide the class into teams. Assign certain points to each color, with purple equaling the most points. The team with the most points wins.

Variation Two: Do not divide the class into teams or assign point values, but give a treat to the students who selects the tube containing the purple dye.

Variation Three: Only use purple dye in select tubes. The rest of the tubes would contain no dye. For this option, you can divide into teams, awarding points when the purple dye is revealed or you can give treats to individuals who find the tubes with purple dye.

1. What does *grudging* mean?
   Answer: Unwillingly or reluctantly; not wanting to do what you are asked to do

2. What was the trade which Thyatira (Lydia's hometown) was famous for?
   Answer: Making purple dye

3. What did the man in the vision ask Paul to do?
   Answer: "Come over into Macedonia, and help us."

4. What were the names of the missionaries who traveled to Macedonia?
   Answer: Paul, Timothy, Silas, and Luke

5. When the missionaries first arrived in Philippi, who welcomed them and invited them to stay in their home?
   Answer: No one

6. Who were the first people the missionaries shared the gospel with in Philippi?
   Answer: A group of women praying by the river

7. Who was the first person to get saved in Philippi?
   Answer: Lydia

8. How did Lydia show hospitality after she trusted in Jesus?
   Answer: She invited the missionaries to stay in her home, and she used her home to help others grow in the Lord.

9. Why could the Israelites relate to strangers?
   Answer: They had been strangers for a long time, as slaves in Egypt.

10. What are some things God has given you that you can use to show hospitality to others?
    Answer: Answers will vary.

Teaching the Memory Verse

1 Peter 4:9

9   Use hospitality one to another without grudging.

Materials Needed

Memory Verse Flashcards from the Ministry Resource download
Pineapple Verse Cards from the Ministry Resource download
Sticker magnets

Set Up

Print 2 sets of the Pineapple Verse Cards from the Ministry
Resource download.

Cut out the pineapples and place magnets on back (for use with
a dry erase board).

On the dry erase board, draw two sets of eight lines (one for
each word of the verse including the reference). There should be one
set of eight lines for each team.

Teaching the Verse

Recite the verse as a class using the Memory Verse Flashcards from
the Ministry Resource download.

Divide the class into two teams in preparation for the memory
verse relay.

Assign one worker for each team who will stand at the front of
the room, and give one set of pineapple verse cards to each. These
can be held at the waist in a fan shape.

To play this relay game, one student from each team walks to
their assigned worker, picks a pineapple verse card containing a
word from the verse, and places the pineapple on the board—on the
correct line of his team's verse.

If the student places a pineapple in the incorrect location, the
next student can fix it and put his own word on the board.

The first team to complete the relay by placing the pineapple
cards in correct order on the board wins.

Note: If you don't have a magnetic board, you can use tape on a
wall, a pocket chart, the base of a chalk board, a table top, etc.

OBJECT LESSON —Pineapples & Hospitality

Materials Needed

Whole pineapple

Pineapple chunks

Toothpicks

Lesson

As you begin teaching this object lesson, pass out pineapple chunks on toothpicks. The pineapple has long been a symbol of hospitality. The story is told that when Christopher Columbus made his second voyage across the Atlantic Ocean, he landed on a Caribbean island where he and his shipmates enjoyed this fruit for their first time.

When Christopher Columbus sailed back to Europe in 1493, he brought back the exotic and sweet pineapple that became very popular and desired by the people. Years later in colonial America, women would place a fresh pineapple as the centerpiece for their tables when hosting visitors in their home. They would often enjoy it for desert after the meal. By this time, the pineapple was symbol of the warmest welcome a hostess could give.

Even today, the pineapple is still a sign to many of kindness, hospitality, and warmth.

Application

Today, we have learned about a lady who showed hospitality long before Christopher Columbus lived and long before the pineapple became an icon symbolizing this good quality! This woman was very kind and generous to members of the early church in the book of Acts, and she was greatly used of God. We should desire to be used of God to be kind to others, just like this woman was!

CRAFT—Lydia Placemat

Supplies

Lydia placemat printable from Ministry
  Resource download
Individual student photos
Contact paper

Instructions

1. Print one 11x17 printable for each student.
2. Take a photo of each student, print, and glue to the center of the printable.
3. Cover with contact paper.

Application

Encourage students to use this placemat throughout the week and to think of ways they can be hospitable and caring to those living inside and outside of their home.

ADDITIONAL RESOURCES

Find the following items on the Ministry Resource download:

- Coloring Page (for younger children)
- Activity Page (for older children)
- Student Take-Home Paper
- PowerPoint Presentation